Experimental Phenomena of Consciousness

Experimental

Phenomena of Consciousness

A Brief Dictionary

Talis Bachmann

Bruno Breitmeyer

Haluk Öğmen

OXFORD

UNIVERSITY PRESS

2007

OXFORD
UNIVERSITY PRESS

Oxford University Press, Inc., publishes works that further
Oxford University's objective of excellence
in research, scholarship, and education.

Oxford   New York
Auckland   Cape Town   Dar es Salaam   Hong Kong   Karachi
Kuala Lumpur   Madrid   Melbourne   Mexico City   Nairobi
New Delhi   Shanghai   Taipei   Toronto

With offices in
Argentina   Austria   Brazil   Chile   Czech Republic   France   Greece
Guatemala   Hungary   Italy   Japan   Poland   Portugal   Singapore
South Korea   Switzerland   Thailand   Turkey   Ukraine   Vietnam

Published by Oxford University Press, Inc.
198 Madison Avenue, New York, New York 10016

www.oup.com

Oxford is a registered trademark of Oxford University Press

Library of Congress Cataloging-in-Publication Data

Bachmann, T. (Talis)
Experimental phenomena of consciousness : a brief dictionary / by Talis Bachmann,
Bruno Breitmeyer, and Haluk Öğmen.
p. cm.
Includes bibliographical references.
ISBN 978-0-19-531690-2
1. Consciousness—Research—Dictionaries.   I. Breitmeyer, Bruno G.
II. Öğmen, Haluk.   III. Title.
BF311.B263 2007
153—dc22   2006023592

1   3   5   7   9   8   6   4   2

Printed in the United States of America
on acid-free paper

Preface

Consciousness is back from obscurity! Treated respectfully by such classic scholars as Wilhelm Wundt, William James, and Edward Titchener, the concept of consciousness virtually disappeared from academic psychology as a research topic for almost a century between the early and late years of the 1900s. However, beginning with the 1980s and 1990s— and not least due to the efforts of an interdisciplinary group of scientists, including Bernard Baars, the late Sir John Eccles, the late Francis Crick, Christof Koch, Gerald Edelman, David Chalmers, Daniel Dennett, Ned Block, John Searle, Patricia Churchland, Nikos Logothetis, Lawrence Weiskrantz, Max Velmans—consciousness returned to the behavioral sciences and reappeared as a respected observational feature of empirical studies. (And the reader, of course, already noticed the Nobel-laureate class of this enterprise.) Top-tier journals such as *Nature* and *Science* started publishing research using *consciousness* (i.e., awareness, explicit reportability) as an experimental variable. Neural correlates of consciousness (NCCs) are a hot topic in brain imaging research. New scientific societies devoted to research on consciousness emerged. New academic journals were launched, such as *Consciousness and Cognition* (Academic Press/Elsevier), *Consciousness and Emotion* (John Benjamins), *PSYCHE* (Association for the Scientific Studies of Consciousness), and *Journal of Consciousness Studies* (Imprint Academic). Universities are again willing to offer special courses on consciousness not only in departments of philosophy but also in the departments of psychology, neurobiology, neuroscience, clinical medicine, and even physics.

Surprisingly, however, the many students in this rehabilitated area of studies, as well as interested laypersons, do not have a succinct handbook or dictionary that would cover the most important experimental phenomena and research paradigms that have become the psychophysical basis for the modern empirical studies of consciousness, let alone many of the "sexy" demonstrations at academic conferences and in the web-based homepages of individual scientists and research laboratories. Laboratory bookshelves and library stocks are empty where there should be something systematic about the empirical phenomena of consciousness. Therefore, the main aim of this book is to provide a first systematic listing and description of the most typical experimental phenomena and effects where consciousness appears as a variable of interest. We describe the names and labels of these phenomena, the principal authors behind the respective research, the basic experimental designs needed to produce them, and a list of useful references and web sites that will help readers to expand and deepen their own knowledge about the topic. We have also constructed a web site that readers can access for demonstrations of some of the key psychophysical techniques and effects used in studies of visual cognition and consciousness.

We had to be quite restrictive, since including most everything that bears on consciousness would have turned our product into another voluminous and unfocused dictionary on psychology and neuroscience, simply because almost everything in psychology is or can be related to consciousness. In some sense, restriction is an honorable task—Sir Winston Churchill once mentioned that the true mark of a gentleman is the capacity of self-restriction. But what should the criteria be for such self-restriction? Fortunately, in the area of modern consciousness research, Bernard Baars, Francis Crick, Christof Koch, and a few others have operationally defined a simple and useful standard for empirical studies of consciousness. One has to find experimental conditions by which invariant stimulation produces variable, multistable states and/or contents of consciousness or, as in the case of many optical illusions, clear discrepancies between what physical stimuli depict and what appears in awareness of these stimuli. In other words, consciousness of an invariant impinging stimulation (the independent variable) appears as a varying dependent variable. This simple principle has become the criterion of choice for our dictionary. We have included experimental phenomena that enjoy sufficiently wide use and that, at the same time, can serve as dependent experimental variables. Additionally, there should be a relatively straightforward and circumscribed set of experimental conditions that are the necessary conditions for a particular phenomenon to emerge. Moreover, from a methodological standpoint, the varying states (e.g., aware versus unaware) or contents (one version of a bistable figure versus another version) of consciousness can, in turn, be used as experimental variables to investigate how they affect behavior. Many of the entries of our dictionary are akin to encyclopedia entries, or mini-articles, with references where necessary (some of them extensive), where the topic is of prime interest to current consciousness researchers. (A list of terms close to the consciousness agenda, but more loosely related to the "consciousness-as-a-variable" criterion, is also added to the main text. An interested reader can easily and independently find explanations for these terms in many dictionaries, handbooks of psychology, neuroscience, philosophy, and the mind, as well as at appropriate web sites.)

The authors have approached the agenda of consciousness from within the same scientific camp and have trod quite similar scientific stepping stones, believing that consciousness has to be studied by the methods of experimental psychology (including psychophysics), combined, whenever possible, with neuroscientific techniques. All three authors have been active in studying visual masking and related spatiotemporal visual phenomena from the combined psychophysical and psychophysiological modeling perspective.

Acknowledgments

We are very much pleased with the efficient and highly professional advice and assistance provided by Catharine Carlin, Nicholas Liu, Stephanie Attia, and their colleagues from Oxford University Press during preparation of this written work. We also thank anonymous reviewers for useful suggestions and Brice Hammack for his help in preparing the accompanying website for the present dictionary (http://www.oup.com/us/consciousness).

Contents

Selection Criteria for Dictionary Terms

- Included are effects and phenomena that have a direct, conscious, experiential counterpart in observers' awareness (or its lack thereof), in comparison with the conditions that provide opposite effects.

- Some theoretical and practical implications of the phenomena and effects are included, where appropriate.

- Excluded are effects that are *behavioristic,* that is, inferential from the experimenter's perspective but not directly experienced by the observer: for example, the von Restorff effect; the Zeigarnik effect; context effects of Palmer, Biederman, Weisstein; no oblique effect, the Stroop effect; the Simon effect, or the Navon effect (global precedence); no refractory period, or the Fehrer-Raab effect.

- No effects depending on thinking and decision-making are included; only sensory, perceptual, and attentional effects (e.g., the Wason selection task effects; effects of subjective frequency; the Valins effect; cognitive dissonance effects; probabilistic judgmental effects; etc.).

- No effects are included that are purely physiological or optical without any psychological, consciousness-related underpinnings or causes (e.g., the motion parallax; the Doppler effect; the Purkinje shift; astigmatism; traumatic analgesia).

- Not included are laws of perception or attention which are inferred from experimental data but not directly experienced by observers (e.g., Ricco's law; Piper's law; Fechner's law; Korte's laws).

- Not included are laws or findings that have the names of their discoverers or formulators, unless there is an experiential, subjective counterpart of the effect that describes perceptual awareness.

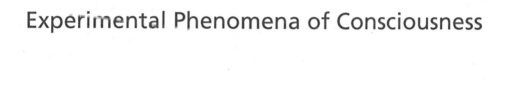

Experimental Phenomena of Consciousness

Dictionary

Abnormal fusion

See *binocular rivalry**.

Ambiguous figures

A very large class of figures (images, drawings), each of which permits two (or sometimes more) alternative perceptual interpretations. At any one time of observing such figures, only one of the alternative interpretations dominates the observer's awareness. Typically, because the alternative perceptual interpretations alternate in the observer's conscious mind, ambiguous figures are often called *reversible figures*. The well-known examples of ambiguous figures have been introduced by Louis-Albert Necker ("Necker cube," 1832) (see Figure 1, left panel), Heinrich Schröder (staircase, 1858), Edwin Boring (W. E. Hill's "My wife and my mother-in-law," 1915, introduced 1930) (see Figure 1, middle panel), Joseph Jastrow ("Duck-rabbit," 1900), B. Bugelsky and D. Alampay ("Rat-man," 1961) (see Figure 1, right panel), Gerald Fisher ("Man-female," 1967), and others. Many famous artists have created astonishingly intriguing examples of pictorial ambiguity in their pictures (e.g., Arcimboldo, Salvador Dali, Maurits Cornelis Escher). Alternation of ambiguous figures has been explained by fatigue or satiation of sensory/perceptual channels, combined with winner-take-all-type competition mechanisms, multistability of the states of the mechanisms of consciousness; by fluctuations in attention; and by the activity of covert exploratory mechanisms of cognitive interpretation. Perceptual interpretation of an ambiguous figure depends considerably on perceptual set and expectancy, perceptual learning and contextual effects. Thus, an invariant object 13 is perceived most probably as the number 13 in the context 12, 13, 14 and as the letter *B* in the context A, 13, C. See also *figure-ground reversal**, *multistability**.

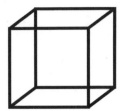

Figure 1

Amodal completion

Consciously experienced perceptual *filling-in** of an occluded region of an object or image. Due to this, an object partly covered by another object and literally providing an explicit view of two pieces of itself is not perceived as separate objects but as one and the same object continuous behind the occluder (in Figure 2, left panel, one sees gray *B*s behind black occluders). When the occluder is removed and only the nonoccluded parts of the objects remain, one tends to see unrelated fragments, and the *B*s are not recognized as readily (see Figure 2, right panel). However, the filling-in also can be more imagery-like or similar to some perceptual inference without a clear and stable sensory quality in it. In these cases, the term *amodal completion* is most applicable. For instance, if a man is lying behind a tree so that only his head and feet are seen without the image of his torso and legs projected onto your retina, one does not perceive separated body parts but a whole, continuous man-object occluded by the features of the tree trunk. The man's body

occluder present   occluder absent

Figure 2

is amodally completed behind the modal visual signals of the tree. The actual signals from the image of the tree compete with the inferred features of a human body and win this competition. The tree is sensed and perceived and becomes what the observer is aware of; the occluded part of the man's body is not directly sensed but nevertheless has become part of what the observer is aware of due to the perceptual context. Conscious perception as inference-making is implied also in the *illusory contour** phenomena and in the *anorthoscopic perception**. See also *filling-in** and *modal completion**.

References

Duensing, S., & Miller, B. (1979). The Cheshire cat effect. *Perception, 8*, 269–273.

Murray, R. F., Sekuler, A. B., & Bennett, P. J. (2001). Time course of amodal completion revealed by a shape discrimination task. *Psychonomic Bulletin and Review, 8*, 713–720.

Ramachandran, V. S. (1992). Blind spots. *Scientific American, 266*, 85–91.

Ramachandran, V. S., & Gregory, R. L. (1991). Perceptual filling in of artificially induced scotomas in human vision. *Nature, 350*, 699–702.

Shipley, T. F., & Kellman, P. J. (Eds.). (2001). *From fragments to objects: Segmentation and grouping in vision*. Amsterdam: Elsevier.

Anorthoscopic perception

Conscious perception of a figure as a whole can occur despite the fact that at any instant of time, only one or a few sections of the figure are revealed (*anorthoscopic presentation*). For instance, a contoured shape of a circle or a camel is moved behind the occluding solid surface that has a vertical slit in it, and only a small part of the whole contour of the shape is directly visible at any time. Nevertheless, observers can recognize whole shapes and report experiencing holistic figures (see Figure 3). Thus, "a camel has gone through the eye of the needle." The perceptual system is capable of spatiotemporal integration despite the fact that only part of the spatial signals reaches the senses at any given instant of time. The phenomenon occurs even when eyes do not move, thus eliminating the explanation based on the so-called *retinal painting theory* (at least for the majority of cases of anorthoscopic perception). The shape of the object should move fast enough to allow meaningful integration in the form of a directly experienced shape, for example, within a fraction of a second. If the picture is too complex and the speed of motion too slow, no holistic meaningful perception occurs (Zöllner, 1862; Hecht, 1924;

Parks, 1965; Haber & Nathanson, 1968; McCloskey & Watkins, 1978; Casco & Morgan, 1984; Fendrich, Rieger, & Heinze, 2005).

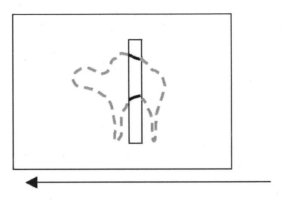

Figure 3

References

Casco, C., & Morgan, M. (1984). The relationship between space and time in the perception of stimuli moving behind a slit. *Perception, 13,* 429–441.

Fendrich, R., Rieger, J. W., & Heinze, H.-J. (2005). The effect of retinal stabilization on anorthoscopic percepts under free-viewing conditions. *Vision Research, 45,* 567–582.

Haber, R. N., & Nathanson, L. S. (1968). Post-retinal storage? Some further observations on Parks' camel as seen through the eye of a needle. *Perception and Psychophysics, 3,* 349–355.

Hecht, H. (1924). Neue Untersuchungen über die Zöllnerschen anorthoskopischen Zerrbilder: Die simultane Erfassung der Figuren. *Zeitschrift für Psychologie, 94,* 153–194.

McCloskey, M., & Watkins, M. J. (1978). The seeing-more-than-is-there phenomenon: Implications for the locus of iconic storage. *Journal of Experimental Psychology: Human Perception and Performance, 4,* 553–564.

Parks, T. E. (1965). Post-retinal storage. *American Journal of Psychology, 78,* 145–147.

Zöllner, F. (1862). Über eine neue Art anorthoscopischer Zerrbilder. *Annalen der Physik und Chemie: Poggendorff's Annalen, 117,* 477–484.

Anthropomorphic perception effect

The perception of intentional causality and human-like interaction in the spatiotemporal physical interactions of simple geometrical forms that themselves do not directly imply or include features of humans or other animate agents. For instance, if a few visual objects like triangles, squares, and rings move relative to each other by approaching, staying close, touching/contacting, moving away, and so forth, then observers spontaneously experience some intentional and animate qualities in these perceived events. One form may seem to chase another, or they may seem to fight; a "big guy" may seem to intimidate a smaller one, and so on. Anthropomorphic perception helps observers to remember much better the succession of changes and movements in a brief animated film compared to when formal physical characteristics of pure distance, motion vectors, and so forth are used (see Heider & Simmel, 1944). See also *phenomenal causallty* *.

Reference

Heider, F., & Simmel, M. (1944). An experimental study of apparent behavior. *American Journal of Psychology, 57*, 243–259.

Apparent motion

See *stroboscopic motion*, phi phenomena, beta motion, induced motion'* and *Duncker effect, motion aftereffect*, Korte's laws, Ternus-Pikler effect*, line motion illusion*, autokinetic motion**.

Aristotle's illusion

The sensory tactile illusion of touching two objects rather than one. Aristotle's illusion appears when an observer closes his or her eyes, crosses two fingers (e.g., index and middle fingers), and then sites a small object in the cleft between the crossed fingers. This was first described by Aristotle in *Parva Naturalia*. Usually, when an observer opens her eyes and visually observes what she touches, the illusion disappears, suggesting that, at least in these circumstances, the visual modality has stronger control over our conscious experiences than tactile modality.

Assimilation

See *brightness assimilation*, color assimilation**.

Attentional blink

Attentional blink (AB) consists in failing to see a second of two targets that are presented at the same display location within a rapid serial visual presentation (RSVP) stream of objects, provided that the first target was successfully and explicitly perceived. The second target usually can be perceived if the first target was not consciously recognized. Thus the attentional blink for a subsequent target typically depends on successful detection of the preceding one. For example, the stream of RSVP objects may consist of letters, and the targets are two numerals. Time intervals between presentation of the successive stream objects are typically in the range of 80–200 ms, and the optimal delay between the second and first target for obtaining the attentional blink is about 200–400 ms. If other stream items are distinctly different from the targets (e.g., alphanumeric symbols versus pictures of objects), AB tends to disappear. When the distractor items in the RSVP-stream are invariant characters, AB may nevertheless be obtained. In the attentional blink, sensory information about both targets is registered within the brain; however, the attentional working-memory analysis of the second target is (temporarily) lacking. Some specific brain areas, such as the anterior cingulate, medial prefrontal cortex, and frontopolar cortex, appear to be important for predicting whether AB occurs or not. See also *repetition blindness**.

References

Bachmann, T., & Hommuk, K. (2005). How backward masking becomes attentional blink: Perception of successive in-stream targets. *Psychological Science, 16*, 740–742.

Broadbent, D. E., & Broadbent, M. H. (1987). From detection to identification: Response to multiple targets in rapid serial visual presentation. *Perception and Psychophysics, 42*, 105–113.

Chun, M. M., & Potter, M. C. (1995). A two-stage model for multiple target detection in rapid serial visual presentation. *Journal of Experimental Psychology: Human Perception and Performance, 21*, 109–127.

Feinstein, J. S., Stein, M. B., Castillo, G. N., & Paulus, M. P. (2004). From sensory processes to conscious perception. *Consciousness and Cognition, 13*, 323–335.

Joseph, J. S., Chun, M. M., & Nakayama, K. (1997). Attentional requirements in a 'preattentive' feature search task. *Nature, 387*, 805–808.

Marcantoni, W. S., Lepage, M., Beaudoin, G., Bourgouin, P., & Richer, F. (2003). Neural correlates of dual task interference in rapid visual streams: An fMRI study. *Brain and Cognition, 53*, 318–321.

Marois, R., Chun, M. M., & Gore, J. C. (2000). Neural correlates of the attentional blink. *Neuron, 28*, 299–308.

Raymond, J. E., Shapiro, K. L., & Arnell, K. M. (1992). Temporary suppression of visual processing in an RSVP task: An attentional blink? *Journal of Experimental Psychology: Human Perception and Performance, 18*, 849–860.

Shapiro, K. (Ed.). (2001). *The limits of attention: Temporal constraints in human information processing.* Oxford: Oxford University Press.

Attentional tracking

A cognitive capacity that allows an observer to consciously keep track of the presence, identity, and features of perceptual objects that were selected for tracking in the presence of the concurrent change of sensory characteristics and features of other competing objects in the visual field. Such tracking can be increased by presenting the selected objects in the left and right visual hemifields, each of which seems to have an independent tracking capacity (Alvarez & Cavanagh, 2005). Tracking is effective even if the features of the selected target-object continuously change (Blaser, Pylyshyn, & Holcombe, 2000.) For example, if a target-disk with a grating-like surface and a certain color is spatially superimposed with another stimulus, and if both of the stimuli begin to gradually change in color and in grating orientation, observers are capable of mentally tracking the continuously changing perceptual quality of the target-object and reporting its feature values at the end of the experimental trial.

It is also possible to track several rigid objects or groups of noncohesive elements simultaneously, but it is difficult to track portions of substances changing their shapes and locations (e.g., in a form of being poured from place to place with dynamic extension and contraction involved).

References

Alvarez, G. A., & Cavanagh, P. (2005). Independent resources for attentional tracking in the left and right visual hemifields. *Psychological Science, 16*, 637–643.

Blaser, E., Pylyshyn, Z. W., & Holcombe, A. O. (2000). Tracking an object through feature-space. *Nature, 408*, 196–199.

Feldman, J. (2003). What is a visual object? *Trends in Cognitive Sciences, 7*, 252–256.

O'Craven, K., Downing, P., & Kanwisher, N. (1999). fMRI evidence for objects as the units of attentional selection. *Nature, 401*, 584–587.

Pylyshyn, Z. W., & Storm, R. W. (1988). Tracking of multiple independent targets: Evidence for a parallel tracking mechanism. *Spatial Vision, 3,* 179–197.
Scholl, B. J. (2001). Objects and attention: The state of the art. *Cognition, 80,* 1–46.
Scholl, B. J., & Pylyshyn, Z. W. (1999). Tracking multiple items through occlusion: Clues to visual objecthood. *Cognitive Psychology, 38,* 259–290.
VanMarle, K., & Scholl, B. J. (2003). Attentive tracking of objects versus substances. *Psychological Science, 14,* 498–504.

Aubert-Fleischl phenomenon (Aubert-Fleischl paradox, Aubert-Fleischl effect)

Subjectively, a moving stimulus appears to move more slowly when tracked by the eyes with smooth pursuit movement, compared with its apparent speed when the eyes are fixated on the background. Discovered by Hermann Ludimar Aubert (1826–1892) and Marxow Ernst Fleischl (1846–1891).

Autokinetic effect (Autokinetic illusion)

In total darkness, a small stationary luminous object gradually appears to move. It is a result of small involuntary eye movements (including nystagmus), the sensory effects of which cannot be compensated for if no visible spatial reference is present. The term was coined by Hermann Aubert (1826–1892). Interestingly, the "feeling" and amplitude of illusory autokinetic motion paradoxically can greatly exceed the small spatial displacement produced by the recorded eye movements. Prolonged visual fixation tends to increase the illusion. The autokinetic effect is susceptible to the influence of social psychological factors, such as conformity in evaluation of perceptual events. Thus, if the luminous dot in darkness is observed by several observers simultaneously, the observers soon reach consensus about how the dot is "moving" (Sherif, 1935).

References

Adams, H. F. (1912). Autokinetic sensations. *Psychological Monographs, 14,* 1–45.
Aubert, H. (1886). Die Bewegungsempfindungen. *Pflüger's Archiv für die Gesamte Physiologie des Menschen und der Tiere, 39,* 347–370.
Levy, J. (1972). Autokinetic illusion: A systematic review of theories, measures and independent variables. *Psychological Review, 78,* 457–474.
Sherif, M. (1935). A study of some social factors in perception. *Archives of Psychology, 27(187),* 1–60.

Baluma-Takete phenomenon

When observers are instructed to decide which one of the two visual objects—one formed from straight lines and appearing "edgy," the other one formed from rounded lines and appearing smooth—is Takete and which one Baluma, they typically respond according to auditory-visual analogy: the one with straight lines and corners appears to be Takete and the smooth one Baluma (see Figure 4). Perceptual smoothness and soft-ness of sound are spontaneously associated with smoothness of visual ap-pearance. This is one of the cross-modal effects. See also *McGurk effect**.

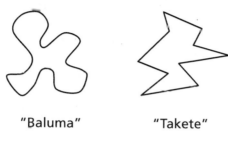

"Baluma"   "Takete"

Figure 4

Reference

Fox, C. W. (1935). An experimental study of naming. *American Journal of Psy-chology, 47,* 545–579.

Benary effect

An example of the dependence of brightness contrast on the placement of an equiluminant spatial region on either a figure or its background (see Figure 5). In the Benary effect, the gray triangle within the black

Figure 5

cross appears brighter compared to the same triangle located outside of the cross and belonging to the background, despite the fact that the local contrast borders of the gray triangle are the same for both of the triangles. This effect was first described by W. Benary in 1924. Also, look for *brightness contrast*, spatial contrast, simultaneous contrast.*

Binocular fusion

Despite the fact that two images of the same object or scene are projected onto disparate, noncorresponding retinal regions of the two eyes, they merge into a single three-dimensional perceptual image in visual awareness. Binocular fusion allows three-dimensional, stereoscopic vision. If the two images differ greatly, *binocular rivalry** occurs instead of binocular fusion.

Binocular rivalry (Retinal rivalry, Dichoptic competition)

When sufficiently different images (of objects, scenes, textures, etc.) are viewed by the two eyes, the images do not blend or fuse in conscious perception but begin to compete or rival one another for conscious registration. If the images are small enough (e.g., less than about 2 deg of visual angle), observers consciously perceive one image at a time, with the two images alternating in awareness. If the images are larger, some parts of one image may combine with some spatially nonoverlapping parts of the other image, producing a characteristic "patching." The image currently in consciousness is termed the dominant one, and the other is the suppressed one. The time periods of dominance fluctuate in an apparently haphazard way, but usually they last in the range of a few seconds. The switching between the eyes is quasi-stochastic and follows a gamma distribution. Typically, the eye that is stimulated with objects in motion (against stationary stimulation), structured stimulation (against nonstructured stimulation), high-contrast stimuli (against low-contrast stimuli), sharp-contoured images (against blurred images), or meaningful stimulation (against meaningless stimulation) tends to dominate in binocular rivalry in terms of the cumulative time of dominance. In the *Cheshire cat effect*, if an observer consciously perceives an object that stimulates one eye (e.g., a stationary image of a smiling cat), and if the other eye is stimulated by a moving object in some area of the otherwise empty visual field for that eye (e.g., a hand is moved over the spatial area corresponding to the body of the cat in the other eye), the observer reports seeing only part of the object (the smiling face of the cat), while the rest of the object (the cat's body) has faded away and is replaced in awareness by the surface color of the empty field. If the competing images are simultaneously presented for a sufficiently short duration (e.g., less than 100 ms), a phenomenon called *abnormal fusion* occurs: both images fuse or blend. Binocular rivalry requires time to become effective.

Modern brain imaging methods (ERPs, fMRI, MEG, microelectrode studies at the cellular level), combined with psychophysical experiments on binocular rivalry, have allowed the study of neural correlates of consciousness (NCCs) in binocular rivalry. Suppression or absence of conscious visibility in binocular rivalry does not mean that the corresponding sensory stimulus is not processed by cortical neuronal units dedicated to encoding visual information. Early sensory representations or at least features of stimulation in the suppressed eye seem to be created or accessed preconsciously but are deprived of access to the later neural mechanisms necessary for conscious experience. The contents (or parts thereof) of conscious perception are encoded from both eyes, but consciousness as such (the conscious accessibility) is alternately generated for the competing stimulus input. In some specific experimental conditions, it can be demonstrated that input from the different eyes (some from the right eye, some from the left eye) combines into a meaningful, consciously apprehended whole following the tendency to form coherent perceptual objects according to expectancy or perceptual skill. Binocular rivalry can be both eye-based (the contents of one eye competing and alternating with the contents of the other) and pattern-based (the contents of one object/interpretation combined from the partial noncorresponding inputs to the two eyes competing with the contents of their remaining combined partial inputs).

Binocular rivalry belongs to the examples of perceptual *multistability**. It was observed already in the early classical observations by Du Tour (in 1760), Sir Charles Wheatstone (1802–1875), Hermann von Helmholtz (1821–1894), and many others. See also *flash suppression effect**.

References

Alais, D., & Blake, R. (Eds.). (2005). *Binocular rivalry.* Cambridge, MA: MIT Press.

Andrews, T. J., & Lotto, R. B. (2004). Fusion and rivalry are dependent on the perceptual meaning of visual stimuli. *Current Biology, 14,* 418–423.

Blake, R., & Logothetis, N. (2002). Visual competition. *Nature Reviews Neuroscience, 3*, 13–23.

Breese, B. B. (1899). On inhibition. *Psychological Monographs, 3*(11), 1–65.

Breese, B. B. (1909). Binocular rivalry. *Psychological Review, 16*, 410–415.

Diaz-Caneja, E. (1928). Sur l'alternance binoculaire. *Annales Oculaire, 165*, 721–731.

Duensing, S., & Miller, B. (1979). The Cheshire cat effect. *Perception, 8*, 269–273.

Grindley, C. G., & Townsend, V. (1965). Binocular masking induced by a moving object. *Quarterly Journal of Experimental Psychology, 117*, 97–109.

Kovács, I., Papathomas, T. V., Yang, M., & Fehér, Á. (1996). When the brain changes its mind: Interocular grouping during binocular rivalry. *Proceedings of the National Academy of Sciences USA, 93*, 15508–15511.

Leopold, D. A., & Logothetis, N. K. (1996). Activity changes in early visual cortex reflect monkeys' percepts during binocular rivalry. *Nature, 379*, 549–553.

Levelt, W. J. M. (1968). *On binocular rivalry.* The Hague: Mouton.

Logothetis, N. K., Leopold, D. A., & Sheinberg, D. L. (1996). What is rivaling during binocular rivalry? *Nature, 380*, 621–624.

Lumer, E. D. (2000). Binocular rivalry and human visual awareness. In T. Metzinger (Ed.), *Neural correlates of consciousness: Empirical and conceptual questions* (pp. 231–240). Cambridge, MA: MIT Press.

Sasaki, H., & Gyoba, J. (2002). Selective attention to stimulus features modulates interocular suppression. *Perception, 31*, 409–419.

Sengpiel, F. (1997). Binocular rivalry: Ambiguities resolved. *Current Biology, 7*, 447–450.

Tong, F., & Engel, S. A. (2001). Interocular rivalry revealed in the human cortical blind-spot representation. *Nature, 411*, 195–199.

Tong, F., Nakayama, K., Vaughan, J. T., & Kanwisher, N. (1998). Binocular rivalry and visual awareness in human extrastriate cortex. *Neuron, 21*, 753–759.

Tononi, G., Srinivasan, R., Russell, D. P., & Edelman, G. M. (1998). Investigating neural correlates of conscious perception by frequency-tagged neuromagnetic responses. *Proceedings of the National Academy of Sciences USA, 95*, 3198–3203.

Walker, P. (1978). Binocular rivalry: Central or peripheral selective processes. *Psychological Bulletin, 85*, 376–389.

Wheatstone, C. (1838). Contributions to the physiology of vision. *Philosophical Transactions of the Royal Society of London. Series B, 128*, 371–394.

Wilson, H. R., Blake, R., & Lee, S.-H. (2001). Dynamics of traveling waves in visual perception. *Nature, 412*, 907–910.

Wolfe, J. M. (1983). Influence of spatial frequency, luminance, and duration on binocular rivalry and abnormal fusion of briefly presented dichoptic stimuli. *Perception, 12*, 447–456.

Wolfe, J. M. (1996). Resolving perceptual ambiguity. *Nature, 380*, 587–588.

Binocular rivalry flash suppression

See *flash suppression effect** and *binocular rivalry**.

Biological motion

Perceptual experience of human body motion created from coherently moving point-light displays. If small light sources (e.g., disks) are attached to the locations of principal joints of a human body and filmed when the person moves in darkness (e.g., walking, running, dancing) then observers who view the film effortlessly and clearly perceive a human body in motion, although what is directly visible are only the few small luminous light sources. The same set of light sources is perceived as a meaningless constellation if presented as a succession of different static displays, as is a moving constellation of light sources that are positioned between the principal joints (e.g., midway between the knee and ankle). Biological motion displays are sufficient for recognizing the characteristic gait or the sex of the person, the ballroom dances danced, the weight of objects lifted, and so forth. Biological motion is an example of the capacity of the perceptual mechanisms to extract *structure from motion*. It stresses the importance of studying event perception in addition to object perception. Seminal works on biological motion include those of Gunnar Johansson (b. 1911).

References

Beintema, J. A., Georg, K., & Lappe, M. (2006). Perception of biological motion from limited-lifetime stimuli. *Perception and Psychophysics, 68,* 613–624.

Giese, M. A., & Poggio, T. (2003). Neural mechanisms for the recognition of biological movements. *Nature Reviews Neuroscience, 4,* 179–192.

Johansson, G. (1973). Visual perception of biological motion and a model for its analysis. *Perception and Psychophysics, 14,* 201–211.

Pavlova, M., Birbaumer, N., & Sokolov, A. (2006). Attentional modulation of cortical neuromagnetic gamma response to biological movement. *Cerebral Cortex, 16,* 321–327.

Troje, N., & Westhoff, C. (2006). The inversion effect in biological motion perception: Evidence for a "life detector"? *Current Biology, 16,* 821–824.

Vaina, L. M., Solomon, J., Chowdhuri, S., Sinha, P., & Belliveau, J. W. (2001). Functional neuroanatomy of biological motion perception in humans. *Proceedings of the National Academy of Sciences USA, 98,* 11656–11661.

Blind spot

See *filling-in** and *amodal completion**.

Blindsight

The capacity of some persons with neurological injuries that create visual scotomas (functionally blind areas within the visual field) to detect and indirectly evaluate visual stimuli that are presented within the blind area. These observers claim that they do not see the objects, but if instructed properly, they may be able to guess some characteristics of the stimuli in the blind field with a probability that exceeds the probability of random guessing. Also, such observers may spontaneously protect themselves from the "invisible" objects thrown toward them in the blind visual field or point correctly to moving objects without claiming to see them. The injuries leading to blindsight typically produce localized damage to the structure and function of the primary cortical visual areas (e.g., V1), or they are due to some lower-level damage (e.g., in the optic radiation fibers projecting from the lateral geniculate body). Blindsight is based on residual information-processing functions mediated by other brain structures, such as the superior colliculus, pulvinar, nonspecific thalamic nuclei, and possibly by some of the spared parts of the injured visual pathways or cortical areas. Blindsight persuasively suggests that since the notion of consciousness is multifaceted, one has to be methodologically careful and precise in founding consciousness research on the reports that an observer produces. For if "blind" observers can produce adaptively reasonable visual responses, then how can we be sure which of the perceptual responses and descriptions of such observers could or could not be produced without concomitant direct visual experience? Also, the concept of perceptual experience itself may become ambiguous and therefore require clear operational definitions (see Pöppel, Held, & Frost, 1973; Weiskrantz, Warrington, Sanders, & Marshall, 1974; Zihl & von Cramon, 1979; Stoerig & Weiskrantz, 1993; Weiskrantz, 1997; de Gelder, de Haan, & Heywood, 2001.)

References

de Gelder, B., de Haan, E., & Heywood, C. (Eds.). (2001). *Out of mind: Varieties of unconscious processes.* Oxford: Oxford University Press.

Pöppel, E., Held, R., & Frost, D. (1973). Residual visual function after brain wounds involving the central visual pathways in man. *Nature, 243,* 295–296.

Stoerig, P., & Weiskrantz, L. (1993). Sources of blindsight. *Science, 261,* 493–495.

Weiskrantz, L. (1997). *Consciousness lost and found: A neuropsychological exploration.* Oxford: Oxford University Press.

Weiskrantz, L., Warrington, E. K., Sanders, M. D., & Marshall, J. (1974). Visual capacity in the hemianopic field following a restricted occipital ablation. *Brain, 97,* 709–728.

Zihl, J., & von Cramon, D. (1979). Restitution of visual function in patients with cerebral blindness. *Journal of Neurology, Neurosurgery, and Psychiatry, 42,* 312–322.

Brightness assimilation

In some appropriate stimulation conditions, the perceived brightness of local, densely spaced, but clearly discriminable visual areas is shifted toward the brightness level of the neighboring local elements (see Figure 6, where the gray surface having identical luminance level appears lighter or darker in brightness depending on whether it is covered with white or black stripes, respectively). Brightness assimilation is the effect that is opposite to *brightness contrast**. If we would gradually increase the size of the stripes in Figure 6, then at some point the assimilation effect changes to a *contrast effect,* where the gray areas between the white stripes appear darker than when between the black stripes. Brightness assimilation tends to be stronger over large areas not captured by focused attention; focused attention tends to emphasize contrast.

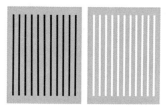

Figure 6

Brightness contrast (Simultaneous brightness contrast, Spatial brightness contrast)

The brightness of an invariant object appears increased if this object is surrounded by or placed adjacent to another stimulus that is darker compared to it; conversely, brightness appears decreased if the neighboring object is brighter. In Figure 7, left panel, the gray central oval appears progressively lighter when it falls within correspondingly less luminous rectangles. To create or maintain spatial brightness contrast, the contours and edges of the stimuli are crucial. Contrast is apparently increased at the border of the areas with different brightness, such as in *Mach bands*, where at the border of a sharp transition from a darker area to a brighter area, the darker seems darker and the brighter seems brighter (introduced by Ernst Mach, 1838–1916.) As the *Craik-O'Brien-Cornsweet effect* shows (see Figure 7, right panel), if luminance gradients of opposite sign are introduced at the borders separating the gray background and two equally gray disks, perceived brightness differences are introduced at the borders and also spread into and fill in the central areas of the two disks, causing one of the equiluminant disks (here, the left one) to appear darker than the other (see Craik, 1940; O'Brien, 1958; Coren, 1969; Cornsweet, 1970; De Valois & De Valois, 1990). See also *Benary effect**, *amodal completion**, *color assimilation**, and perceptual *filling-in**.

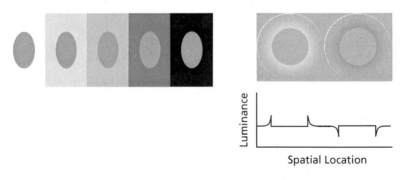

Figure 7

References

Coren, S. (1969). Brightness contrast as a function of figure-ground relations. *Journal of Experimental Psychology, 80,* 517–524.

Cornsweet, T. N. (1970). *Visual perception.* New York: Academic Press.

Craik, K. J. W. (1940). The effect of adaptation on subjective brightness. *Proceedings of the Royal Society of London. Series B, Biological Sciences, 128,* 232–247.

De Valois, R. L., & De Valois, K. K. (1990). *Spatial vision.* Oxford: Oxford University Press.

O'Brien, V. (1958). Contour perception, illusion, and reality. *Journal of the Optical Society of America, 48,* 112–119.

Broca-Sulzer effect

The perceived brightness of an equiluminant stimulus depends on the duration of the stimulus. Too brief or too long stimuli appear dimmer than stimuli with optimum duration. For sufficiently bright objects in the photopic range, the optimum duration for the perceived maximum brightness ranges from 40 to 120 ms. To obtain a distinct Broca-Sulzer effect, visual stimuli should have sharp (not blurred) spatial edges. In the closely related *Brücke-Bartley effect,* the stimulus that flickers at roughly a 10Hz frequency seems brighter than an equiluminant steady stimulus.

References

Bowen, R. W., & Pokorny, J. (1978). Target edge sharpness and temporal brightness enhancement. *Vision Research, 18,* 1691–1696.

Broca, A., & Sulzer, D. (1902). La sensation lumineuse fonction du temps. *Journal de Physiologie et de Pathologie Generale, 4,* 632–640.

Bruner and Goodman effect

The apparent size of objects can be influenced by their subjective value: observers tend to overestimate the size of coins according to their nominal value, although this effect is absent when cardboard disks with sizes identical to those of coins are used for evaluation (Bruner & Goodman, 1947). Higher level cognitive factors interact with early level sensory-perceptual processes. The exact mechanisms that are responsible for this effect are still unclear.

Reference

Bruner, J. S., & Goodman, C. C. (1947). Value and need as organizing factors in perception. *Journal of Abnormal and Social Psychology, 42,* 33–44.

Cai and Schlag effect

In this illusory effect, a horizontally moving bar gradually changes size and, at some point along its trajectory, also changes to a different color for one frame. In perceptual experience, the new color is assigned to a different-sized bar at a spatial location ahead of its actual spatial location (i.e., shifted in the direction of motion). In the experimental setup used to generate this effect, a visual object is presented in successive frames so that its spatial position is gradually changed (as if moving in a given direction, e.g., from left to right). The size of the object also is gradually changed by clearly discriminable increments from frame to frame. In one of the frames, the color of the object changes, for example, from green to red and then back to green for the remaining following frames. The task of observers is to evaluate the spatial position of the object's color change. Given optimum speed of motion and size increments, a subjective mislocalization of the position of the color change in the direction of motion occurs virtually without fail. Most importantly, the changed color of the physically smaller object is subjectively associated with the form and locus of a larger object appearing at an advanced position in the direction of motion. Sensory features of color, location, and size are misbound in an integrated perceptual object. The mechanisms responsible for this effect are most probably closely associated with the processes involved in the *perceptual asynchrony effect**. See also *feature binding, illusory conjunctions**.

References

Cai, R. H., & Schlag, J. (2001a). Asynchronous feature binding and the flash-lag illusion. *Investigative Ophtalmology and Visual Science, 42,* S711.

Cai, R., & Schlag, J. (2001b). A new form of illusory conjunction between color and shape [Abstract]. *Journal of Vision, 1*(3), 127a.

Change blindness

The inability to consciously notice substantial changes in images or scenes despite the illusory perceptual experience that everything is seen. Typically, this occurs when two otherwise identical images of scenes which differ only in terms of the presence or characteristics of an object or feature alternate at an optimum rate, and a blank gap between the successive images is included. Despite this, the introspective experience of the successive exposures is one of fullness, clarity, and unchanged character of the whole scene. For instance, if one of the two engines of a jet plane in an airport scene disappears and reappears under the wing between the frames, observers may not notice this change for a quite substantial duration (e.g., tens of seconds). However, if the nature and/or location of change is preliminarily known or expected, observers notice it virtually immediately. Properly directed selective attention and attenuation of internal noise in the perceptual processing system lead to increased awareness of the locus and nature of the change. A typical optimum timing of the stimulation events for change blindness are as follows: first frame for 0.4 s, blank interval for 0.2 s, second frame for 0.4 s, blank interval for 0.2 s, first frame again for 0.4 s, and so forth. Change blindness also can happen in real-life scenes—for example, if an interviewer briefly leaves the interview setting and on return is replaced by another person, the interviewed observer may not notice this change. In a related phenomenon, disruptions and pauses up to 600 ms inserted into videotaped ongoing events that are attentively monitored go mostly unnoticed. The change blindness phenomenon indicates that conscious experience is set to aid perception of the events and scenes as holistic spatiotemporal entities with the function of representing the main gist or essence of the situation and not necessarily its details in toto.

References

Levin, D. T., & Varakin, D. A. (2004). No pause for a brief disruption: Failures of visual awareness during ongoing events. *Consciousness and Cognition, 13,* 363–372.

O'Regan, J. K., Rensink, R. A., & Clark, J. J. (1999). Change-blindness as a result of "mudsplashes." *Nature, 398,* 34.

Rensink, R. A. (2002). Change blindness. *Annual Review of Psychology, 53,* 245–277.

Rensink, R. A., O'Regan, J. K., & Clark, J. J . (1997). To see or not to see: The need for attention to perceive changes in scenes. *Psychological Science, 8,* 368–373.

Simons, D. J., & Levin, D. T. (1997). Change blindness. *Trends in Cognitive Sciences, 1,* 261–267.

Simons, D. J., & Levin, D. T. (1999). Failure to detect changes to people during a real-world interaction. *Psychonomic Bulletin and Review, 5,* 644–649.

Wilken, P., & Ma, W. J. (2004). A detection theory account of change detection. *Journal of Vision, 4,* 1120–1135.

Cheshire cat effect

See *binocular rivalry**.

Cocktail party effect (Cocktail party phenomenon)

The ability of a listener to attend to one among several simultaneous conversations, leading to the awareness of the attended messages and a lack of full awareness of the competing messages. Various selective attention cues such as spatial direction of the messages, selective voice characteristics, personal relevance of the conversation topic or words (e.g., one's own name) help to determine what is selected by attention for awareness. The term was introduced by Colin Cherry (1914–1979) in 1957. The cocktail party phenomena helped to develop theoretical discussions and experimental research in selective attention by pioneers in the field, such as Donald Broadbent, Neville Moray, and Anne Treisman, among others. The classic experimental method, *dichotic listening**, was used most often to conduct more precise research on the ability of attentional selection among several competing sensory messages. In dichotic listening, two mutually different and simultaneous streams of messages are presented to an observer over earphones—one stream to the right ear, the other to the left ear. Observers are able to consciously monitor one stream of the messages according to the input channel (e.g., the left ear) while at the same time remaining unaware of the substantial contents of the other channel (e.g., the right ear). The standard control for assuring that observers attend to one of the streams is the so-called shadowing technique, where observers have to continuously report what they have just heard over the attended ear.

Cohene and Bechtoldt effect

A subtype of visual *masking**, where a meaningless smaller subset of spatially localized visual stimuli remains present after another subset of spatially localized stimuli is switched off from the whole stimulus: the longer-lasting meaningless subset exerts a backward-masking effect on the full set, comprising a meaningful stimulus so that its form and meaning cannot be consciously perceived. This experimental procedure, termed the "simultaneous onset–asynchronous offset technique," was systematically introduced by Cohene and Bechtoldt (1974, 1975). Typically, a stimulus object like a pair of letters is formed by superimposing sets of small dots so that part of the dots are arranged in a shape of letters (see Figure 8, where the bigram *CV* is formed). This superimposed set including the letters is presented for a brief time (e.g., 50 ms), and then part of the dots is switched off so that a meaningless constellation of the remaining dots is present for some additional duration (e.g., 100 ms). Although no new stimulus input is added to the display, the remaining part of the dots acts as a vigorous backward mask of the prior target letters. This effect shows that backward masking cannot be explained solely on the basis of a mask's energy relative to that of a target and that the mechanisms of conscious perception are relatively slow, thus emphasizing the crucial role of trailing rather than leading stimulation (see Bachmann, 1994, and DiLollo, Enns, & Rensink, 2000, for two explanations of this regularity). Subsequently, Vincent DiLollo, James Enns, and their associates have expanded the simultaneous onset–asynchronous offset technique to other types of stimuli, such as Landolt-C targets masked either by surrounding rings or even by four-dot masks that do not fully surround the target. Delayed offset masking is especially strong when spatial attention is not focused on the target and mask location. See also *masking**, *substitution masking*.

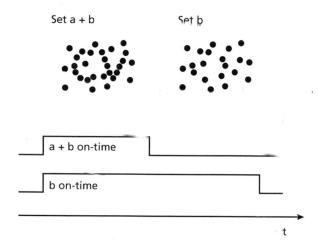

Figure 8

References

Bachmann, T. (1994). *Psychophysiology of visual masking: The fine structure of conscious experience*. Commack, NY: Nova Science.

Cohene, L. S., & Bechtoldt, H. P. (1974). Visual recognition as a function of stimulus offset asynchrony and duration. *Perception and Psychophysics, 15*, 221–226.

Cohene, L. S., & Bechtoldt, H. P. (1975). Visual recognition of dot-pattern bigrams: Extension and replication. *American Journal of Psychology, 88*, 187–199.

DiLollo, V., Bischof, W. F., & Dixon, P. (1993). Stimulus-onset asynchrony is not necessary for motion perception or metacontrast masking. *Psychological Science, 4*, 260–263.

DiLollo, V., Enns, J. T., & Rensink, R. A. (2000). Competition for consciousness among visual events: The psychophysics of reentrant visual processes. *Journal of Experimental Psychology: General, 129*, 481–507.

Enns, J. T., & DiLollo, V. (1997). Object substitution: A new form of masking in unattended visual locations. *Psychological Science, 8,* 135–139.

Enns, J. T., & DiLollo, V. (2000). What's new in visual masking? *Trends in Cognitive Sciences, 4,* 345–352.

Color assimilation

Similar to *brightness assimilation*,* in color assimilation the color of a given region of a multicolored display takes on or assimilates with the color of neighboring regions. In Figure 9, the diagonally arrayed square elements reflect identical wavelengths of light yet are perceived to have different colors depending on whether they are assimilated into adjoining regions defined by the neighboring yellow versus blue squares. Color assimilation is the opposite of *color contrast* (see Figure 10).

Figure 9

Reference

Fach, C., & Sharpe, T. (1986). Assimilative hue shifts in color gratings depend on bar width. *Perception and Psychophysics, 40,* 412–418.

Color contrast (Simultaneous color contrast, Spatial color contrast)

Color contrast occurs when two backgrounds that reflect clearly different wavelengths surround stimuli that reflect the same wavelengths. Typically, the shift in apparent color of a test pattern tends toward the color that is complementary to the background color. For instance, in Figure 10, blue and yellow backgrounds surround two mirror-symmetric test patterns, both of which are the same gray. The test patterns, however, appear to have different colors, the left one tending toward yellow, and the right one tending toward blue. These effects are explained in terns of the *opponent-process* theory of color vision first introduced by Hering (1878) and subsequently elaborated, among others, by Hurvich and Jameson (1957) and De Valois (1960; see De Valois, 1965).

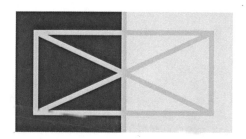

Figure 10

References

De Valois, R. L. (1965). Behavioral and electro-physiological studies of primate vision. In W. D. Neff (Ed.), *Contributions to sensory physiology* (Vol. 1, pp. 137–178). New York: Academic Press.

Hering, E. (1878). Zur Lehre vom Lichtsinn. Vienna: Gerold.

Hurvich, L. M. & Jameson, D. (1957). An opponent-process theory of color vision. *Psychological Review, 64*, 384–404.

Color-phi phenomenon

In a *stroboscopic motion** display, when the first flashed object has a different color from the second, apparent motion is accompanied by a smooth change of the perceived color of the apparently moving object.

Reference

Kolers, P. A., & von Grünau, M. (1976). Shape and color in apparent motion. *Vision Research, 16*, 329–335.

Color spreading

A variety of the illusory phenomena where a subjective color or hue of an area spreads perceptually onto a neighboring region of space, such as some surface or object, filling it in. It may happen in the case of the blind spot, the area of which is perceptually filled in by the color of the surrounding area; in the case of the assimilation effect; and in the case of illusory contours or surfaces (e.g., *neon color spreading* or the van Tuijl effect). In Figure 11, left panel, the central part appears like a purple striped belt with a hazy film of purple color rather than a succession of distinctly separate vertical lines with clear white regions between them. Color spreading also occurs in the "watercolor" illusion (Pinna, Brelstaff, & Spillmann, 2001). When one chromatic contour is flanked by different chromatic contours, the flanking colors spread into the area enclosed by them. In Figure 11, right panel, the region labeled *A* appears as though faint orange bled into it, the region labeled *B* appears a faint bluish, and the region labeled *C* transforms in the rightward direction from a faint orange to a bluish tint. See also *modal completion**, *color assimilation**, *illusory contours**, *filling-in**.

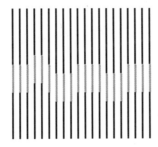 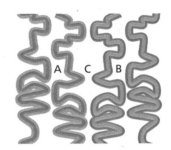

Figure 11

References

Pinna, B., Brelstaff, G., & Spillmann, L. (2001). Surface color from boundaries: A new "watercolor" illusion. *Vision Research, 41,* 2669–2676.
van Tuijl, H. F. M. J. (1975). A new visual illusion: Neonlike color spreading and complementary color induction between subjective contours. *Acta Psychologica, 39,* 441–445.

Complementary afterimage

In the complementary afterimage, color appears as the complementary color of the stimulus, the viewing of which leads to the perception of complementary afterimage after the stimulus has been withdrawn from sight. For instance, fixating the black dot between the blue and orange diamond shapes in Figure 12, left panel, for 20 s or so and then fixating the black dot in the middle of the light-gray rectangle allows one to experience diamond-like illusory afterimages that do not look like the original stimulus but have the complementary color qualities (an orange-and-blue hue). When an achromatic stimulus is used to induce the afterimage, we may say that the complementary afterimage of the stimulus, for example, a white diamond, is its negative afterimage, for instance, a gray diamond. This can be seen by fixating the black dot in the white diamond surrounded by the dark-gray rectangular field for a while and then fixating the black dot in the middle of the larger light-gray rectangle. Now, fixate the black dot in the center of the white diamond surrounded by an orange rectangle on the far right of Figure 12 for a while, and then fixate the black dot in the middle of the larger light-gray rectangle. You should see a rectangular afterimage that appears blue, that is, the complement of orange, enclosing a diamond-shaped afterimage that looks orange, which is *not* the complement of white. How does this happen? Like *spatial* or *simultaneous color contrast** (see Figure 10), these effects can be explained in terms of *opponent-process* theories of chromatic vision combined with spatial opponency, like that also evidenced by *brightness contrast**. See also *afterimage, successive contrast.*

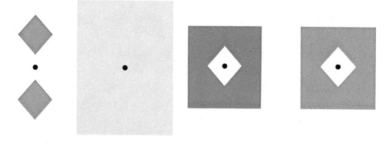

Figure 12

Contrast (Contrast effect)

A family of effects consisting in the intensification or emphasis of feature differences produced by the spatial juxtaposition of stimuli. Contrast effect appears most characteristically between such properties of stimuli, objects, or regions as their size or intensity (e.g., leading to perceived size, brightness, or loudness differences) or their shape and quality (e.g., leading to subjective shape, color, or timbre differences). In *simultaneous contrast**, the juxtaposed stimuli are presented simultaneously (e.g., Figure 7). In *successive contrast,* the juxtaposed stimuli or experiences are presented or appear one after another. In many cases of simultaneous contrast, the effects are based on the mechanisms of *lateral inhibition* at the different stages of sensory information processing such as in the retina, in the visual or auditory cortex, and so forth. Various sensory or perceptual *aftereffects* also show contrast effects (e.g., see Figure 12 as a variety of *successive color contrast*). Examples of the *simultaneous brightness* and *color contrast* are shown in Figures 7 and 10. *Size contrast effects* are evident in the Ebbinghaus size illusion, shown in Figure 26, right panel. See also *Mach bands, fading effects*, illusions*, afterimages**.

Covert spatial attention effect

The main mechanism that enables us to select important visual objects and locations for the best possible observation and detailed analysis consists in selective eye movements. Observers move their eyes so as to fixate on objects of interest, thus guaranteeing that the optical images of these objects fall onto the central part of the retina which has the best spatial resolution (the area called *fovea;* the process of fixation is often termed *foveation* of object images). *Saccadic eye movements* and visual fixations *that* are maintained periodically after such movements are in the service of *overt spatial visual attention.* Typically, what is fixated by one's gaze is perceived most distinctively and stands out saliently as the focus of visual attention. Yet, in addition to the overt orienting of the gaze, observers are capable of deliberately changing the direction and focus of spatial attention without the corresponding eye movements. This capability is commonly termed *covert spatial attention.* While fixating on the word *covert* in the title of this entry, you can deliberately and selectively shift to the word afterimages located above and thereby enhance its perceived clarity or distinctiveness. At the same time, however, it is difficult to attend to the capital letter *Y* in the word *Yet* a few lines below. But if readers switch their selective covert spatial attention to *Y*, the other stimuli in other spatial locations become more difficult to perceive, including the former target stimulus *covert.* Covert spatial attention has been given several metaphorical names such as *mind's eye, spotlight, searchlight, zoom lens,* and so forth (cf. the works of John Jonides, Charles Eriksen, Michael Posner, and Francis Crick). This phenomenon was known already over a century ago to early classic investigators such as H. von Helmholtz, W. Wundt, and W. James. About 100 to 150 ms are required to form a new attentional focus in response to the onset of a cue at or near the new location, and the subjective resolution of stimulus detail is inversely related to the spatial size of the covert focus of attention (the larger the focused area, the less the resolution). If covert spatial attention is reoriented by symbolic (*central*) cues, such as small arrows, the number code of a clock face, or geographical symbols (East, West, . . .), more time is required for the covert attention to focus on the new spatial location (i.e., about 250–400 ms). See also *pop-out effect**.

Covert object/feature attention effect

We can also covertly orient our attention to objects or features of an object. This capability is commonly termed *covert object/feature attention*: those features of an object display that one attends to can significantly affect what one perceives. Figure 13 shows a version of the Müller-Lyer illusion. The horizontal distances between the vertices *a* and *b* and between *b* and *c* are identical. Yet attending to the blue vertices of the display should yield the impression that the distance between *a* and *b* is longer than that between *b* and *c*. Conversely, attending to the red vertices of the display should yield the impression that the distance between *a* and *b* is shorter than that between *b* and *c*.

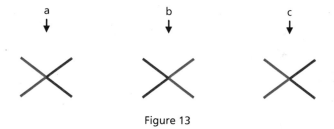

Figure 13

Crawford effect

See *masking**.

Crowding effect

A stimulus that is clearly visible and discriminable if presented in isolation may become unrecognizable to conscious perception if presented in the context of other spatially neighboring stimuli (e.g., distractor objects). In Figure 14, while one fixates on the black dot on the left, it is not difficult to experience the visual outline qualities of the isolated letter *K* to the right. However, if the same letter stimulus located at the same distance from fixation is presented among other letters that are *crowding* the display area, it becomes barely discriminable. It has been shown that information about the subjectively indiscriminable features of the crowded stimuli can be processed preconsciously by the brain (He, Cavanagh, & Intriligator, 1996; He & MacLeod, 2001). It is most likely that the inaccessibility to consciousness of the features of the crowded objects owes much less to the limits of sensory mechanisms of feature detection and discrimination than to the limits of attentional resolution and/or insufficient level of activity of the mechanisms which enable conscious access to the preconsciously processed visual information. Excessive *feature integration* (see also *feature misbinding*), whereby features of the distractors are incorrectly integrated with those of the target items, may also underlie the crowding effect. In the earlier studies of this effect, the term *lateral masking* was often used (e.g., see Bouma, 1970).

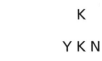

Figure 14

References

Bouma, H. (1970). On the nature of input channels in visual processing. *Nature, 226,* 177–178.

He, S., Cavanagh, P., & Intriligator, J. (1996). Attentional resolution and the locus of visual awareness. *Nature, 383,* 334–337.

He, S., Cavanagh, P., & Intriligator, J. (1997). Attentional resolution. *Trends in Cognitive Sciences, 1,* 115–121.

He, S., & MacLeod, D. I. A. (2001). Orientation-selective adaptation and tilt aftereffect from invisible patterns. *Nature, 411,* 473–476.

Huckauf, A., & Heller, D. (2004). On the relations between crowding and visual masking. *Perception and Psychophysics, 66,* 584–595.

Intriligator, J., & Cavanagh, P. (2001). The spatial resolution of visual attention. *Cognitive Psychology, 43,* 171–216.

Levi, D. M., Hariharan, S., & Klein, S. A. (2002). Suppressive and facilitatory spatial interactions in peripheral vision: Peripheral crowding is neither size invariant nor simple contrast masking. *Journal of Vision, 2,* 167–177.

Pelli, D. G., Palomares, M., & Majaj, N. J. (2004). Crowding is unlike ordinary masking: Distinguishing feature integration from detection. *Journal of Vision, 4,* 1136–1169.

Põder, E. (2006). Crowding, feature integration, and two kinds of "attention." *Journal of Vision, 6,* 163–169.

Rajimehr, R., Vaziri-Pashkam, M., Afraz, S.-R., & Esteky, H. (2004). Adaptation to apparent motion in crowding condition. *Vision Research, 44,* 925–931.

Cutaneous rabbit phenomenon

When a series of taps are applied successively at different locations along the arm (separated by as much as many dozens of centimeters), with inter-tap intervals in the range of 50–200 ms, and the whole train lasts for about a second or slightly more, observers experience an illusory traveling of the taps in regular sequence over equidistant points along the arm. The feeling is similar to the one that would emerge in awareness if a little animal were hopping along the arm. See also *stroboscopic motion*, Czermak effect*, illusion*.*

References

Flach, R., & Haggard, P. (2006). The cutaneous rabbit revisited. *Journal of Experiemental Psychology: Human Perception and Performance, 32,* 717–732.
Geldard, F. A., & Sherrick, C. E. (1972). The cutaneous "rabbit": A perceptual illusion. *Science, 178,* 178–179.

Czermak effect

A tactile variety of apparent motion, described by Johann Czermak in 1855. When two locations of skin are successively and repeatedly stimulated with an optimum time interval between the stimulations (e.g., 100 ms), the observer perceives one tactile stimulus moving back and forth instead of perceiving two different sensations produced by two different tactile stimuli. The Czermak effect is a form of tactile apparent motion which shares several psychophysical regularities with visual *stroboscopic motion** (Kirman, 1974). See also *cutaneous rabbit*.*

Reference

Kirman, J. H. (1974). Tactile apparent movement: The effects of interstimulus onset interval and stimulus duration. *Perception and Psychophysics, 15,* 1–6.

Depth reversal effects

See *ambiguous figures*, figure-ground reversal*, multistability*.*

Dichotic listening effects

When two sequences of mutually different auditory stimuli are simultaneously presented to the two ears, one to the right ear and the other sequence to the left ear, listeners typically perceive and can report the contents of only one sequence but not the other. It is possible to switch to the other ear, but at the expense of losing awareness for the contents presented to the ear from which attentional monitoring just has been withdrawn. The standard experimental control over whether the observer indeed perceives the contents of the selected channel (e.g., words presented to the left ear) consists in online repeating of the words from the attended channel aloud, a procedure called *shadowing*. Listeners usually cannot report the stimuli from the unattended channel except when the series is terminated and the observer is immediately instructed to report the contents of the unattended channel. With the aid of immediate auditory memory, one—or at most a few—of the stimuli from the end of the unattended series often can be reported. Introspective experience indicates that the very last items in the unattended list have been held available for few seconds in a kind of *echoic* memory without conscious apprehension of their meaning being briefly accessible upon a proper instruction or cuing. It is fair to say that not all characteristics of the stimuli in the unattended channel in dichotic listening remain totally unnoticed. For example, termination of the succession of words, sudden and substantial change in the physical characteristics of the input (such as switching from a soft male voice to a loud female voice), and some other very salient changes can be detected by the listeners. Since the seminal work by Colin Cherry (1953), the technique of dichotic listening often has been used for studying selective auditory attention, especially as related to the theoretical problem regarding the stage of information processing where selection takes place—either closer to the input, based on physical characteristics of the stimuli, or closer to the output, based on semantic contents and response-related decision-making (e.g., see the works of Broadbent, Moray, and Treisman). The need to abandon the radical input-selection theories was stressed by some notable experimental findings: sometimes listeners involuntarily switch to the unattended channel, provided that a highly relevant meaningful stimulus appears there (e.g., the listener's own name); if a word formerly associated with an unpleasant conditioning stimulus (e.g., electric shock) or its close semantic associate is presented among neutral items in the unattended channel remaining out of awareness, it still evokes a stress-related galvanic skin reaction. These and similar observations mean that relatively high-level processing should be performed on the signals that enter the unattended channel, including the stimuli that listeners remain unaware of (see, e.g., Gray & Wedderburn, 1960; Corteen & Wood, 1972; von Wright, Anderson, & Stenman, 1975.) See also *cocktail party phenomenon**.

References

Broadbent, D. E. (1958). *Perception and communication.* London: Pergamon.

Broadbent, D. E. (1971). *Decision and stress.* London: Academic Press.

Cherry, E. C. (1953). Some experiments on the recognition of speech with one and two ears. *Journal of the Acoustic Society of America, 25,* 975–979.

Corteen, R. S., & Wood, B. (1972). Autonomic responses to shock-associated words in an unattended channel. *Journal of Experimental Psychology, 94,* 308–313.

Gray, J. A., & Wedderburn, A. A. (1960). Grouping strategies with simultaneous stimuli. *Quarterly Journal of Experimental Psychology, 12,* 180–184.

Moray, N. (1959). Attention in dichotic listening: Affective cues and the influence of instructions. *Quarterly Journal of Experimental Psychology, 11,* 56–60.

Moray, N. (1969). *Attention: Selective processes in vision and hearing.* London. Hutchinson.

Scharf, B. (1998). Auditory attention: The psychoacoustical approach. In H. Pashler (Ed.), *Attention* (pp. 75–117). Hove, England: Psychology Press.

Treisman, A. M. (1960). Contextual cues in selective listening. *Quarterly Journal of Experimental Psychology, 12,* 242–248.

Treisman, A. M. (1969). Strategies and models of selective attention. *Psychological Review, 76,* 282–299.

von Wright, J. M., Anderson, K., & Stenman, U. (1975). Generalisation of conditioned G.S.R.s in dichotic listening. In P. M. A. Rabbitt & S. Dornič (Eds.), *Attention and performance V.* (pp. 194–204). London: Academic Press.

Duncker effect

See *induced motion effects**.

Duration effects

Typically, in the *filled duration illusion**, observers overestimate durations of time intervals if these intervals are filled with more information-processing content (events, variety of experiences, more complex stimulation) compared to *empty* or uneventful (nonvarying) time intervals. When observers judge the speed with which time seems to have passed, the more eventful time intervals appear as if their time flow has been faster. Up to a point, increased attention to an event also increases its perceived duration, as do increases in the level of arousal and excitement of the perceiver. For example, previously briefly presented objects appear to have a shorter duration when they are presented again as compared to newly presented and equally brief stimuli that demand more attention. If effort-consuming attention is directed away from the event or stimulation, the duration of which has to be judged, the judgments tend to be shorter. However, with quite difficult tasks that demand intense concentration, time seems to pass faster, leading to underestimation of duration. In the *time-order error*, the first one of the two successive time intervals of equal duration is judged as being shorter. In the time-interval or temporal *production* tasks (compared to *evaluation* tasks, where perceptual judgment is used), more cognitive processing leads to the underestimation of time passed during the production of the necessary intervals. With speeded subjective flow of time, the moment when a predesignated time interval seems to have passed arrives more quickly. Time flow in general seems to become faster with increasing age of the person.

References

Allan, L. G., & Kristofferson, A. B. (1974). Psychophysical theories of duration discrimination. *Perception and Psychophysics, 16*, 26–34.

Brown, S. W. (1985). Time perception and attention: The effects of prospective versus retrospective paradigms and task demands on perceived duration. *Perception and Psychophysics, 38*, 115–124.

Fraisse, P. (1963). *The psychology of time.* New York: Harper & Row.

Michon, J. A., & Jackson, J. L. (1985). *Time, mind and behavior.* Berlin: Springer.

Mo, S. S. (1971). Judgment of temporal duration as a function of numerosity. *Psychonomic Science, 24*, 71–72.

Ornstein, R. (1975). *On the experience of time.* Harmondsworth, England: Penguin.

Thomas, E. A. C., & Weaver, W. B. (1975). Cognitive processing and time perception. *Perception and Psychophysics, 17*, 363–367.

Witherspoon, D., & Allan, L. G. (1985). The effect of a prior presentation on temporal judgments in a perceptual identification task. *Memory and Cognition, 13*, 101–111.

Zakay, D. (1993). Time estimation methods: Do they influence prospective duration estimates? *Perception, 22*, 91–101.

Zakay, D., Nitzan, D., & Glicksohn, J. (1983). The influence of task difficulty and external tempo on subjective time estimation. *Perception and Psychophysics, 14,* 451–456.

Emmert's law (Emmert effect)

This law states that the perceived size of an afterimage is directly proportional to its perceived distance. For instance, when a visual *afterimage* is viewed against a surface that is relatively close to the observer, it appears smaller than when it is viewed against a surface located to a more distant position. The reader can test this with the help of Figure 12 by creating the afterimage and then viewing it against a distant wall rather than on the page containing the figure. Discovered by the Italian scientist Benedetto Castelli (1578–1643) and systematically studied and described by the Swiss ophthalmologist and psychophysicist Emil Emmert (1844–1911).

References

Emmert, E. (1881). Grössenverhältnisse der Nachbilder. *Klinische Monatsblätter für Augenheilkunde, 19,* 443–450.
Epstein, W., Park, J., & Casey, A. (1961). The current status of the size-distance hypothesis. *Psychological Bulletin, 58,* 491–514.

Fading effects

For a variety of visual effects, sensory stimulation, provided that it is unchanging and/or highly predictable and poor, tends to disappear (fade away) from perceptual experience. The fading phenomena include the fading of *stabilized* retinal *images** (e.g., Riggs, Ratliff, Cornsweet, & Cornsweet, 1953; Pritchard, Heron, & Hebb, 1960; Krauskopf, 1963; Yarbus, 1967; Ditchburn, 1973), the *Troxler effect,* the *Ganzfeld effect**, and *semantic satiation**. Fading phenomena are explained by sensory *adaptation* effects or by higher level cognitive effects related to the influence of redundancy reduction on the activity of the mechanisms of conscious experience. Also, they can be linked to fatigue or conflict in the workings of the attention processes. An example of (at least partial) fading due to a (semi)stabilized image is shown in Figure 15. When fixating the central dot for a few or few dozen seconds, the blurred image tends to fade somewhat and/or shrink in size or even disappear. Fading is typically accompanied by *filling in**.

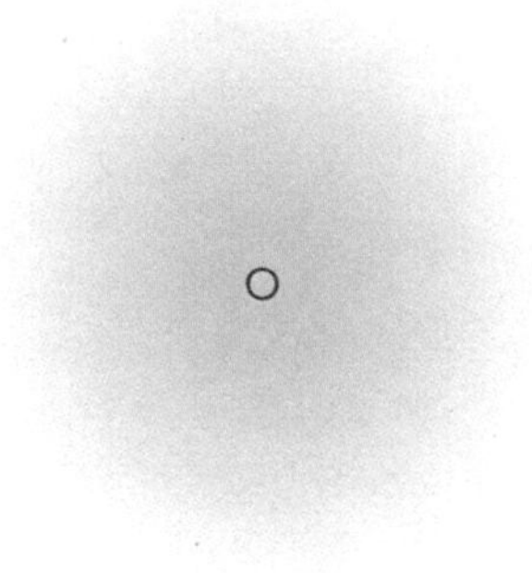

Figure 15

References

Ditchburn, R. W. (1973). *Eye-movements and visual perception*. Oxford: Oxford University Press.

Gerrits, H. J. M., DeHaan, B., & Vendrik, A. J. H. (1966). Experiments with retinal stabilized images: Relations between the observations and neural data. *Vision Research, 6,* 427–440.

Krauskopf, J. (1963). Effect of retinal image stabilization on the appearance of heterochromatic targets. *Journal of the Optical Society of America, 53,* 741–744.

Pritchard, R. M., Heron, W., & Hebb, D. O. (1960). Visual perception approached by the method of stabilized images. *Canadian Journal of Psychology, 14,* 67–77.

Riggs, L. A., Ratliff, F., Cornsweet, J. C., & Cornsweet, T. N. (1953). The disappearance of steadily fixated visual test objects. *Journal of the Optical Society of America, 43,* 495–501.

Stürzel, F., & Spillmann, L. (2001). Texture fading correlates with stimulus salience. *Vision Research, 41,* 2969–2977.

Troxler, D. (1804). Über das Verschwinden gegebener Gegenstände innerhalb unseres Gesichtskreises. In K. Himly & J. A. Schmidt (Eds.), *Ophtalmische Bibliothek. II.2* (pp. 1–119). Jena, Germany: Friedrich Frommann.

Welchman, A. E., & Harris, J. M. (2001). Filling-in the details on perceptual fading. *Vision Research, 41,* 2107–2117.

Yarbus, A. L. (1967). *Eye movements and vision*. New York: Plenum.

Feature attribution

Under certain conditions, visual features belonging to one stimulus can be perceived as belonging to another stimulus. The occurrence of this illusion in *feature misbinding,* the *Cai and Schlag effect*,* or *illusory conjunctions** is interpreted to reflect errors of the perceptual system stemming from its processing limits. If one inserts a feature, such as a vernier offset, to one of the elements in the *Ternus-Pikler** display, this feature can be perceived as belonging to another element. This non-retinotopic attribution of features follows the rules of perceptual grouping in the Ternus-Pikler display. Contrary to feature misbinding or illusory conjunctions, feature attribution is not viewed as an error stemming from the limitations of the visual system. Rather, it appears to reflect an active process whereby features are attributed to objects according to rules of perceptual grouping. See also *feature inheritance**.

Reference

Otto, T. U., Öğmen, H., & Herzog, M. H (2006). The flight path of the phoenix: The visible trace of invisible elements. *Journal of Vision, 6,* 1079–1086.

Öğmen, H., Otto, T. U., & Herzog, M. H. (2006). Perceptual grouping induces non-retinotopic feature attribution in human vision. *Vision Research, 46,* 3234–3242.

Feature inheritance

It is possible to arrange spatial and temporal characteristics of two brief successive visual objects so that the first object remains out of awareness and the following object, which is consciously perceived, inherits certain features of the invisible (backward-masked) object. Consequently, the second stimulus is perceived to have characteristics belonging to the first. In a typical stimulus display, where feature inheritance can be observed, a so-called *vernier stimulus* (two small vertical lines slightly offset from collinearity) is presented first, followed immediately by a spatially overlapping grating formed from collinearly arranged pairs of vertical lines (i.e., without vernier offset; see Figure 16). The vernier is pre-

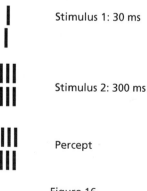

Stimulus 1: 30 ms

Stimulus 2: 300 ms

Percept

Figure 16

sented, for example, for 30 ms, and the grating, for example, appears for 300 ms. As a result, observers perceive illusory vernier offset of the elements of the following grating; the illusory perceptual effect is most distinct at the end of the grating. The spatial distance between the invisible vernier stimulus that induces the illusion and the locus of the end of grating where the illusion is most distinct can amount to about 0.3 deg of the visual angle. Other features that can be inherited in this way are line orientation and line motion. See also *feature attribution*, masking**.

Reference

Herzog, M. H., & Koch, C. (2001). Seeing properties of an invisible object: Feature inheritance and shine-through. *Proceedings of the National Academy of Sciences USA, 98,* 4271–4275.

Feature misbinding

See *illusory conjunctions**.

Figural aftereffects

A figural distortion of perception of a visual stimulus (e.g., a line, form, or grating) resulting from observing (usually for a relatively prolonged period) a prior visual stimulus (see also *adaptation, illusions*, tilt aftereffect, successive contrast*). Figure 17 shows one such aftereffect, called the *curvature aftereffect*. To experience this effect, convince yourself first that the left grating is straight and vertical; next, fixate the region around the *x* in the right curved grating for about 30–60 s; then shift your gaze to the *x* on the left grating. You should experience the formerly straight-appearing lines as having a slight curvature opposite to that of the curved lines in the right grating. Figural aftereffects are thought to be due to selective adaptation of neural processes tuned to various features of a figure, such as its curvature, orientation, spatial frequency, and so on.

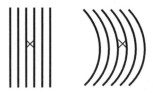

Figure 17

References

Barlow, H. B., & Hill, R. M. (1963). Evidence for a physiological explanation of the waterfall illusion and figural after-effects. *Nature, 200,* 1345–1347.

Blakemore, C., & Nachmias, J. (1971). The orientation specificity of two visual after-effects. *Journal of Physiology, 213,* 157–174.

Coltheart, M. (1971). Visual feature-analyzers and aftereffects of tilt and curvature. *Psychological Review, 78,* 114–121.

Gibson, J. J., & Radner, M. (1937). Adaptation, after-effect and contrast in the perception of tilted lines. *Journal of Experimental Psychology, 20,* 453–467.

Sutherland, N. S. (1961). Figural after-effects and apparent size. *Quarterly Journal of Psychology, 13,* 222–228.

Figure-ground reversal

Numerous types of visual stimuli exist where a physically invariant stimulus (figure, shape, drawing, picture) allows variable (alternating, shifting) perceptual interpretations (see *ambiguous figures**, perceptual *multistability**). These types of figures are ambiguous because they permit variable, often mutually incompatible, interpretation in terms of the meaning or physical specification of the depicted object. In one such type, thoroughly studied by Gestalt psychologists, the contour that makes a borderline between a central area and its background is perceived at times as belonging to the central part and at times as belonging to the surrounding part. This may lead to alternative perceptions where what was a figure becomes background and vice versa. For instance, in Figure 18, the central part at times appears in awareness as

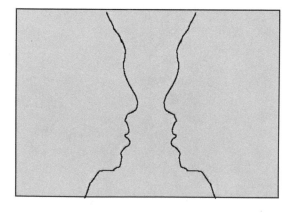

Figure 18

a vase (with the rest providing a background) and at times as a background for two faces in profile looking at each other. Figure-ground reversal typically implies depth reversal in terms of which part of the image appears to be located at a depth plane closer to the observer and which part appears more distant. In consciousness, it is virtually impossible to hold alternative interpretations simultaneously. A lot of research on figure-ground reversal was inspired by the work of Danish Gestaltist Edgar Rubin. See also *binocular rivalry**, *dichotic listening**.

Filled-duration illusion

A specified period of time is experienced as longer when many events fill it compared to a period of time of equal duration which includes considerably fewer events or is empty. See also *duration effects**.

Filled-space illusion

A spatial region appears larger if it is occupied by a number of separate elements than if it is empty (see Figure 19).

Figure 19

Filling-in

A variety of visual phenomena most often described under the umbrella concepts of *amodal completion** and *modal completion**. Typically, filling-in involves processes by which an attribute that is not present at a specific (e.g., spatial) locus or that cannot be mediated by stimulation of corresponding sensory receptors is inferred from the immediately surrounding context and attributed to stimulation from that locus. Best exemplified is our inability to experience an empty area or scotoma that should emerge as a result of some optical information falling onto the *blind spot* of the retina. (Each retina contains a small area, where the fibers of the optic nerve leave the eye, which lacks visual receptors and therefore is *technically blind*.) Despite the blind spot, we do not see an empty hole in our visual field; the area of the visual field that corresponds to the blind spot is filled with the sensory attribute(s) characterizing the immediate surrounding. Figure 20 can be used for a demonstration of the filling-in of the blind spot. Cover your left eye, and fixate the black cross located to the left of the black disk. While maintaining fixation, move the book slowly back and forward (you may also have to tilt it slightly) until you find the distance that allows the image of the black disk to fall on the blind spot. You notice this by the disappearance of the disk from your perception and by the accompanying experience of the white background filling in the area located at the place of blind spot. You do not experience a hole in the white background.

Perceptual completion can be quite intelligent by filling in the occluded or insensitive area with what is suggested by the contents of the directly visible stimulation (Ramachandran & Gregory, 1991; Ramachandran, 1992). For example, if two aligned bars have a gap in between them, and if this gap is projected onto the blind spot, observers report seeing a continued long bar without a gap in it. Similarly, colors of a surface, textures, and regular patterns with many local elements can be filled in. On the other hand, more complex features like letters of a word or the head of an animal cannot be completed (filled-in) with the quality of a vivid sensory experience. Thus, perceptual completion can be very vivid and clear, as in the examples of color or texture just referred to. Filling-in can occur also for the artificial, experimentally induced scotomas and scotomas that result from injuries. Beside *color extrapolation,* filling-in can involve *brightness extrapolation* and *surface completion.* See also *color spreading*, illusory contours*, fading effects*.*

Figure 20

References

Caputo, G. (1998). Texture brightness filling-in. *Vision Research, 38,* 841–851.

Churchland, P. S., & Ramachandran, V. S. (1996). Filling-in: Why Dennett is wrong. In K. Akins (Ed.), *Perception* (pp. 132–157). Oxford: Oxford University Press.

de Weerd, P., Gattass, R., Desimone, R., & Ungerleider, R. G. (1995). Response of cells in monkey visual cortex during perceptual filling-in of an artificial scotoma. *Nature, 377,* 731–734.

Gerrits, H. J. M., & Vendrik, A. J. H. (1970). Simultaneous contrast, filling-in process and information processing in man's visual system. *Experimental Brain Research, 11,* 411–440.

Komatsu, H. (2006). The neural mechanisms of perceptual filling-in. *Nature Reviews Neuroscience, 7,* 220–231.

Paradiso, M. A., & Hahn, S. (1996). Filling-in percepts produced by luminance modulation. *Vision Research, 36,* 2657–2663.

Paradiso, M. A., & Nakayama, K. (1991). Brightness perception and filling-in. *Vision Research, 31,* 1221–1236.

Pessoa, L., & de Weerd, P. (Eds.). (2004). *Filling-in: From perceptual completion to skill learning.* Oxford: Oxford University Press.

Pessoa, L., Thompson, E., & Noë, A. (1998). Finding out about filling-in: A guide to perceptual completion for visual science and the philosophy of perception. *Behavioral and Brain Sciences, 21,* 723–802.

Ramachandran, V. S. (1992). Filling in gaps in perception: I. *Current Directions in Psychological Science, 1,* 199–205.

Ramachandran, V. S., & Gregory, R. L. (1991). Perceptual filling-in of artificially induced scotomas in human vision. *Nature, 350,* 699–702.

Zur, D., & Ullman, S. (2003). Filling-in of retinal scotomas. *Vision Research, 43,* 971–982.

Flash-lag effect

In one form of this illusion, a feature of an object (e.g., its location) changes continuously over time. At a given instant, a neighboring object is briefly flashed, so that its feature value is identical to the temporally synchronous feature value of the continuously changing object. Observers experience that the flashed object lags behind the temporally synchronous feature value of the continuously changing object. For instance, if a moving object continuously changes its location and another similar object is briefly flashed at a position aligned with the moving object, the flashed one appears to lag behind, a phenomenon called *flash-lag effect* (FLE) (see Figure 21).

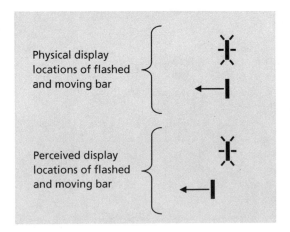

Figure 21

In the moving-object version of FLE, for the flashed object to appear subjectively aligned with the moving object, the flashed one must be presented at a critical location corresponding to the one reached by the moving object about 20–80 ms *later* than the flashed one. FLE also appears in conditions where both objects appear simultaneously, but the stationary object is quickly switched off while the moving one continues to be presented in motion. Because of FLE, if a light source that is mounted onto a solid plate is flashed stroboscopically (with an optimal frequency and very short duration) while the plate is rotating, the light source appears at a location on the plate not corresponding to its physical location. FLE also can be obtained with a moving object that briefly appears within a spatial aperture (window) that is very small relative to the distance covered by the continuously moving object. Although the direction and speed of motion of the moving but briefly viewed object are equal to those of the continuously moving object, the FLE is distinctly experienced, provided that the spatial extent of the aperture and the speed of motion yield an exposure of less than about 100–200 ms. The longer this exposure, the smaller the spatial and/or temporal value of the FLE. The magnitude and sign of the FLE depend critically on the relative luminance values of the flashed and the moving objects. An increase in the luminance of the flashed (moving) object causes a decrease (increase) in the magnitude of the effect. When the flashed object is much brighter than the moving one, the flashed object is perceived to lead, rather than lag, the moving object. FLE also can be obtained with other continuously changing features, such as color, spatial frequency, brightness, and texture characteristics, as well as with nonvisual stimuli (e.g., auditory, tactile).

Significantly, in another form of the FLE, it is not necessary that a feature change occurs in the continuous object before the flashed object: FLE also can be obtained if an invariant stimulus (e.g., the letter *I*) is presented as a stream at the same spatial location and a target-object (e.g., the letter *Z*) is flashed both within the stream and outside of the stream. In these conditions, the in-stream target of the two simultaneous targets appears to have been presented before the out-of-stream, isolated target. Thus what seems to be critical in FLE is some temporal continuity in the exposure of the accumulating sensory input and not a feature change per se. The FLE demonstrates that, in general, objects presented in streaming sensory input appear in consciousness faster than objects that are presented in isolation de novo. Explanations for this effect include differential latencies, temporal facilitation, motion extrapolation, position persistence, stimulus-triggered updating of internal models, stimulus-triggered sampling of neural activity, and masked priming. See also *Hess effect**, *Fröhlich effect**, *representational momentum**.

References

Alais, D., & Burr, D. (2003). The "flash-lag" effect occurs in audition and cross-modally. *Current Biology, 13,* 59–63.

Bachmann, T., Luiga, I., Põder, E., & Kalev, K. (2003). Perceptual acceleration of objects in stream: Evidence from flash-lag displays. *Consciousness and Cognition, 12,* 279–297.

Bachmann, T., & Põder, E. (2001). Change in feature space is not necessary for the flash-lag effect. *Vision Research, 41,* 1103–1106.

Baldo, M. V. C., Kihara, A. H., Namba, J., & Klein, S. A. (2002). Evidence for an attentional component of the perceptual misalignment between moving and flashing stimuli. *Perception, 31,* 17–30.

Brenner, E., & Smeets, J. B. J. (2000). Motion extrapolation is not responsible for the flash-lag effect. *Vision Research, 40,* 1645–1648.

Chappell, M., Hine, T. J., & Hardwick, D. (2002). The flash-lag effect and equiluminance. *Clinical and Experimental Ophthalmology, 30,* 213–216.

Eagleman, D. M. (2001). Visual illusions and neurobiology. *Nature Reviews Neuroscience, 2,* 920–926.

Eagleman, D. M., & Sejnowski, T. J. (2000). Motion integration and postdiction in visual awareness. *Science, 287,* 2036–2038.

Hine, T. J., White, A. M. V., & Chappell, M. (2003). Is there an auditory-visual flash-lag effect? *Clinical and Experimental Ophthalmology, 31,* 254–257.

Ishii, M., Seekkuarachchi, H., Tamura, H., & Tang, Z. (2004). 3D flash lag illusion. *Vision Research, 44,* 1981–1984.

Kanai, R., & Verstraten, F. A. J. (2006). Visual transients reveal the veridical position of a moving object. *Perception, 35,* 453–460.

Khurana, B., Watanabe, K., & Nijhawan, R. (2000). The role of attention in motion extrapolation: Are moving objects "corrected" or flashed objects attentionally delayed? *Perception, 29,* 675–692.

Kreegipuu, K., & Allik, J. (2004). Confusion of space and time in the flash-lag effect. *Perception, 33,* 293–306.

Krekelberg, B., & Lappe, M. (2001). Neuronal latencies and the position of moving objects. *Trends in Neurosciences, 24,* 335–339.

Mackay, D. M. (1958). Perceptual stability of a stroboscopically lit visual field containing self-luminous objects. *Nature, 181,* 507–508.

Metzger, W. (1932). Versuch einer gemeinsamen Theorie der Phänomene Fröhlichs und Hazeloffs und Kritikihrer Verfahren zur Messung der Empfindungszeit. *Psychologische Forschung, 16,* 176–200.

Nijhawan, R. (1994). Motion extrapolation in catching. *Nature, 370,* 256–257.

Nijhawan, R. (2002). Neural delays, visual motion and the flash-lag effect. *Trends in Cognitive Sciences, 6,* 387–393.

Öğmen, H., Patel, S. S., Bedell, H. E., & Camuz, K. (2004). Differential latencies and the dynamics of the position computation process for moving targets, assessed with the flash-lag effect. *Vision Research, 44,* 2109–2128.

Schlag, J., & Schlag-Rey, M. (2002). Through the eye slowly: Delays and localization errors in the visual system. *Nature Reviews Neuroscience, 3,* 191–200.

Sheth, B. R., Nijhawan, R., & Shimojo, S. (2000). Changing objects lead briefly flashed ones. *Nature Neuroscience, 3,* 489–495.

Watanabe, K., Nijhawan, R., Khurana, B., & Shimojo, S. (2001). Perceptual organization of moving stimuli modulates the flash-lag effect. *Journal of Experimental Psychology: Human Perception and Performance, 27,* 879–894.

Whitney, D., Murakami, I., & Cavanagh, P. (2000). Illusory spatial offset of a flash relative to a moving stimulus is caused by differential latencies for moving and flashed stimuli. *Vision Research, 40,* 137–149.

Flash-suppression effect (Flash-suppression illusion)

If an observer views a visual stimulus presented to one eye, and after a while another stimulus is briefly flashed to the other eye (stimulating the area spatially overlapping with the location of the competing stimulus), the newly presented stimulus becomes consciously perceived, and the former one, despite being continuously presented, becomes suppressed from awareness. This phenomenon is known as *binocular rivalry flash suppression* (Wolfe, 1984). Although such suppression produced by a single flash in the other eye is transient, it can be prolonged by continuously flashing different images rapidly to the other eye (Tsuchiya & Koch, 2005). When the same flash is presented also to the eye viewing the continuously presented stimulus, *generalized flash suppression* is induced (Wilke, Logothetis, & Leopold, 2003). A different version of the effect could be termed *specific flash suppression* (Breitmeyer & Rudd, 1981; Kanai & Kamitani, 2003). Here the flashed stimuli are spatially designed to specifically take out existing target stimuli. Novelty in the input to the perceptual system captures conscious-perception resources and dominates over the already known information in awareness.

See also *binocular rivalry*, masking**.

References

Breitmeyer, B. G., & Rudd, M. (1981). A single-transient masking paradigm. *Perception and Psychophysics, 30,* 604–606.

Kanai, R., & Kamitani, Y. (2003). Time-locked perceptual fading induced by visual transients. *Journal of Cognitive Neuroscience, 15,* 664–672.

Kreiman, G., Fried, I., & Koch, C. (2002). Single-neuron correlates of subjective vision in the human medial temporal lobe. *Proceedings of the National Academy of Sciences USA, 99,* 8378–8383.

Sheinberg, D. L., & Logothetis, N. K. (1997). The role of temporal cortical areas in perceptual organization. *Proceedings of the National Academy of Sciences USA, 94,* 3408–3413.

Tsuchiya, N., & Koch, C. (2005). Continuous flash suppression reduces negative afterimages. *Nature Neuroscience, 8,* 1096–1101.

Wilke, M., Logothetis, N. K., & Leopold, D. A. (2003). Generalized flash suppression of salient visual targets. *Neuron, 39,* 1043–1052.

Wolfe, J. M. (1984). Reversing ocular dominance and suppression in a single flash. *Vision Research, 24,* 471–478.

Flicker fusion

If the temporal frequency of a stroboscopically flickering (intermittent or fluctuating) light is set at a sufficiently high value called the *critical flicker frequency* (CFF), observers do not experience the alternation of the separate flashes but instead see a more or less steady or continuous light. As one gradually increases the temporal frequency of stimulation, the initial perceptual experience of alternation of light and dark transforms at and above the CFF into a continuously visible luminous stimulation. CFF depends on the state of light adaptation, on intensity and background contrast of the periodic stimuli, and on the spatial size (area) of the flickering stimulus. At intermediate and high (photopic) light adaptation levels, the CFF typically has a value of about 40 Hz (40 cps). In the central, foveal region of the visual field, flicker fusion is obtained at lower temporal frequencies than in the peripheral regions. (Temporal resolution of the peripheral visual channels is better.) Obtaining a steady or fused light impression from television, computer, or motion picture displays would be impossible without flicker fusion. The refresh rates of the television and computer screens, where actually luminous and dark states alternate, are set at 50–60 Hz, which is sufficient to have a more or less stable impression of a steady light.

References

Kelly, D. H. (1972). Flicker. In D. Jameson & L. M. Hurvich (Eds.), *Handbook of sensory physiology: Visual psychophysics* (Vol. 7, pp. 273–302). New York: Springer.

Scharf, B. (Ed.). (1975). *Experimental Sensory Psychology.* Glenview, IL: Scott, Foresman.

Form from motion

Form from motion, like *biological motion**, is another example of *structure from motion*. Much like form from stereo-depth, random-dot displays, each of which alone reveals no structure or form, can reveal a moving form that is based purely on spatial displacements of successive frames of the random dot-displays. This use of random-dot cinematograms was also developed by Bela Julesz and staff of Bell Telephone Laboratories. It is also found in nature and is the principle of natural camouflage—or, rather, *de-camouflage*. Figure 22 shows a photo of some little frogs on a tree trunk. The texture of the frogs matches that of the bark and moss on which the animals are resting. As long as the frogs do not move, they remain pretty well hidden from both predator and prey, which has some definite advantages. However, were they to move, their form would become much

Figure 22

more visible (decamouflaged) to predator and prey alike. Form from motion is based on the Gestalt organizational principle of *common fate*.

References

Braddick, O. J. (1974). A short-range process in apparent motion. *Vision Research, 14,* 519–527.

Braddick, O. J. (1980). Low-level and high-level processes in apparent motion. *Philosophical Transactions of the Royal Society B, 290,* 137–151.

Chang, J. J., & Julesz, B. (1983). Displacment limits of spatial frequency filtered random-dot cinematograms in apparent motion. *Vision Research, 23,* 1379–1385.

Julesz, B., & Bosche, C. (1966). *Studies of visual texture and binocular depth perception. A computer-generated movie series containing monocular and binocular movies.* Murray Hill, NJ: Bell Telephone Laboratories.

Form from stereo-depth

Two random-dot displays, each of which alone reveals no structure or form, can reveal a cyclopean, stereoscopic form that is based purely on binocular image disparity. This use of random-dot stereograms was discovered by Bela Julesz of Bell Telephone Laboratories and is the basis of a variety of autostereograms which have become popular viewing material in recent times. Autostereograms, like the one shown in Figure 23,

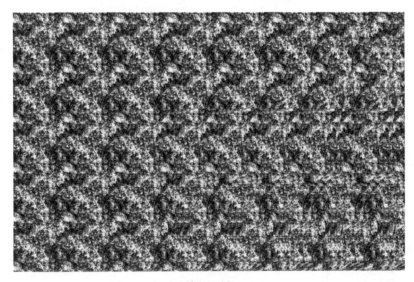

Figure 23

do reveal a somewhat repetitive texture structure; however, they also conceal a cyclopean form unless and until the autostereogram is viewed in such a way as to activate binocular-disparity processing mechanisms. If one looks at Figure 23 and crosses or diverges one's eyes until the two white squares in the autostereogram display fuse, a horse-like form should eventually become visible. With divergence, the horse should appear as an object in front of a background. With crossing of the eyes, it should appear like a horse-shaped hole in a foreground.

References

Julesz, B. (1971). *Foundations of Cyclopean Perception*. Chicago: University of Chicago Press.

Tyler, C. W., & Clarke, M. B. (1990). The autostereogram. *SPIE Stereoscopic Displays and Applications, 1258*, 182–196.

Fröhlich effect

If a moving object appears from behind an occluder (e.g., a plate, surface, or another object), its perceived initial location is not at the border of the occluder edge but at a location spatially advanced in the direction of motion (Fröhlich, 1923). The faster the speed of motion, the larger the illusory spatial displacement is. It seems as if a moving object suddenly appearing from behind an occluder is registered in awareness with a delay, causing its perceived position to correspond not to its initial position but rather to a position physically ahead on its trajectory. See also *flash-lag effect*, Hess effect*, representational momentum*, anorthoscopic perception**.

References

Fröhlich, F. W. (1923). Über die Messung der Empfindungszeit. *Zeitschrift für Sinnesphysiologie, 54*, 58–78.

Kerzel, D., & Gegenfurtner, K. R. (2004). Spatial distortions and processing latencies in the onset repulsion and Fröhlich effects. *Vision Research, 44*, 577–590.

Kirschfeld, K., & Kammer, T. (1999). The Fröhlich effect: A consequence of the interaction of visual focal attention and metacontrast. *Vision Research, 39*, 3702–3709.

Müsseler, J., & Aschersleben, G. (1998). Localizing the first position of a moving stimulus: The Fröhlich effect and an attention-shifting explanation. *Perception and Psychophysics, 60*, 683–695.

Müsseler, J., Stork, S., & Kerzel, D. (2002). Comparing mislocalizations with moving stimuli. The Fröhlich effect, the flash-lag effect and representational momentum. *Visual Cognition, 9,* 120–138.

Galli effect

If brief visual and auditory pulsed stimuli are presented alternately in rapid succession, observers often report an experience of a blended audiovisual perception of a "lighted sound" or "audible light." In some cases, observers reported having perceived a "tunnel of light that grows longer or shrinks down along with how a sound travels in it" or as simply "something that moves between the sound and light." The effect was reported by P. Galli in 1932. See also *synesthesia**.

Ganzfeld effects

After more or less prolonged viewing (e.g., more than 3–4 min) of a special type of a uniformly illuminated visual field lacking any discriminable features, contours, depth cues, luminance- and color-gradients (i.e., a *Ganzfeld,* German for "whole field"), observers begin to experience a variety of illusory phenomena. The surface quality of the visual field disappears, and a fog-like entity is experienced. Eventually, the perceived color of the homogeneous Ganzfeld stimulus fades away from experience, turning into a gray, featureless entity (*Eigengrau* in German); many observers experience perceptual *blankout,* a feeling of being unable to see. Sometimes, subjective blackening of the visual field or its becoming dark gray occurs in observers' awareness. Also, hallucinatory shapes and a flight of colors can be experienced. Rapid and apparently instantaneous restoration of color experience and noticing of a stimulus occurs if a visible object or shadow is introduced as a newly appearing stimulus into the Ganzfeld. Eye movements may temporarily restore color experience in the Ganzfeld. Switching off the actual color of the Ganzfeld display can cause perception of the complementary color, similar to the perception of a *complementary afterimage.* This suggests that sensory adaptation is going on in the feature channels at preconscious levels, that is, without the adapting stimulus being experienced in awareness. The Ganzfeld effects also suggest that, for perceptual experience, spatial and temporal changes of stimulation contents are necessary. Natural conditions that may lead to experiences close to Ganzfeld effects include snow blindness or arctic whiteout, during which the visual field is filled mostly with a uniform and contourless environment, or during high-altitude flights, when similarly only a spatially uniform sky fills the visual field.

References

Avant, L. L. (1965). Vision in the Ganzfeld. *Psychological Bulletin, 64,* 246–258.

Hochberg, J., Triebel, W., & Seaman, G. (1951). Color adaptation under conditions of homogeneous stimulation (ganzfeld). *Journal of Experimental Psychology, 41,* 153–159.

Koffka, K. (1935). *Principles of Gestalt psychology.* New York: Harcourt Brace.

Metzger, W. (1930). Untersuchungen am Ganzfeld: II. Zur Phänomenologie des homogenen Ganzfelds. *Psychologische Forschung, 13,* 6–29.

Weintraub, D. J. (1964). Successive contrast involving luminance and purity alterations of the Ganzfeld. *Journal of Experimental Psychology, 68,* 555–562.

Generalized flash suppression

See *flash suppression effect*, fading effects*,* and *binocular rivalry*.*

Geometric illusions

See *illusions*.*

Hallucination

A nonveridical perceptual experience resulting not from the stimulation of sense organs but as a result of a hallucinogenic brain state. These states may be a result of the influence of hallucinogens (substances like LSD, psilocybin, etc.), hypnotic states, prolonged deprivation of sensory input or of sleep, schizophrenia, or some neurological disorders. Substantial doses of alcohol can produce hallucinations; observers suffering from alcoholic delirium often experience this. Hallucinations are neither *illusions** nor dreams. They are pathological effects and/or symptoms. In a true hallucination, an observer perceives the hallucinatory scenes and objects as if they are real. In pseudohallucination, what is perceived is not confused with actually existing entities—the observers understand that what they experience is a result purely of their own mind without any corresponding source of external stimulation.

Halo effect

Usually, the term halo effect is used in the context of social or personal attribution as the tendency of biased rating or evaluation of some individual: for example, when an individual has created an impression of being good (or bad), this may bias ratings or evaluations of some other, actually unrelated characteristics of the same individual (e.g., intelligence). In the context of conscious-perception phenomenology, halo effect has a different meaning. In some experimental conditions, a perceived object or feature appears as having a glowing aura or halo around it, although in terms of objective physical sensory input, the corresponding luminance and/or color of the spatial areas which surround the object do not include corresponding luminance or color gradients. Perceptual halo effect may emerge in dichoptic *masking** if, for instance, as depicted in Figure 24, one eye is stimulated with a flash of a large dark homogeneous square and the other eye with a flash of a small black square on a bright yellow background. Given proper timing of the flashes, the observer may consciously perceive a small black square on the background of a large dark square, with the immediate surrounding of the small square appearing as a halo of bright yellow which gradually becomes darker at greater distances from the small square until it melts into the dark of the large gray area. Halo effects also can be observed in simultaneous contrast, Mach bands, *binocular rivalry**, *afterimages**, and some other types of visual display. For example, a dark negative afterimage that appears as a result of prolonged staring at a bright object appears as having a bright ring around it; this illusory halo in the vicinity of the dark afterimage appears brighter than the rest of the surrounding area. See also *Stoper and Mansfield effect**.

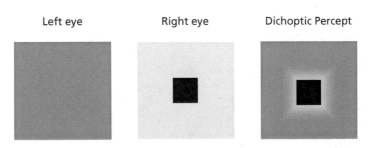

| Left eye | Right eye | Dichoptic Percept |

Figure 24

Hermann grid

A special type of inducing stimulus that creates illusory dark patches to appear at the intersection of white stripes on a dark background or vice versa; for this effect to be experienced most strongly, the intersections should be viewed *parafoveally,* or in the periphery (see Figure 25). If any of the intersections is foveated, the effect disappears or diminishes greatly at that location. Hermann grid illusion is based on the processes of lateral inhibition within the neuronal circuits possessing center-surround organization of receptive fields. The effect was introduced by a German physiologist Ludimar Hermann (1838–1914) in 1870. See also *illusory contours*.*

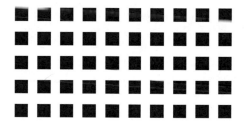

Figure 25

Hess effect

When two spatially aligned objects of different luminous intensity move as a tandem (e.g., along the horizontal trajectory), the more luminous one appears to lead the dimmer one as if being spatially shifted forward in the direction of motion. See also *flash-lag effect*, Pulfrich effect*, Fröhlich effect*.*

References

Hess, C. V. (1902). Untersuchungen über den Erregungsvorgang im Sehorgan bei kurz- und bei längerdauernder Reizung. *Pflügers Archiv für Gesamte Physiologie, 101,* 226–262.

Williams, J. M., & Lit, A. (1983). Luminance dependent visual latency for the Hess effect, the Pulfrich effect, and simple reaction time. *Vision Research, 23,* 171–179.

Illusions

In general terms, illusions are generated by physiological and/or psychological processes yielding in awareness phenomenal properties of an object or scene which are noticeably discrepant from their physical or factual properties. Illusions involve misconception, misperception, or misrepresentation. The term illusion comes from Latin (1) *illusio* or *illusionis,* deceit, or (2) *illudere,* to mock or play *(ludere).* A feeling of success can be an illusion, provided that objective evidence shows something else. Traditionally, however, the scientific use of the concept of illusion is most often related to sensory/perceptual distortions or nonveridicalities. In some theoretical conceptualizations, conscious experience in principle is interpreted as a grand illusion, and much of what humans can perceive and can be aware of is considered to be, to a large extent, illusory (Dennett, 1991, 2001; Noë, 2002; Noë, Pessoa, & Thompson, 2000; O'Regan, 1992, 2002). Although this approach is intriguing, and although brains and minds tend to create illusions, pan-illusionism of the human conscious mind inevitably leads to radically skeptic and agnostic conclusions that can hardly be accepted.

All senses are susceptible to illusory experiences where the objective characteristics and/or properties of the physical stimuli (colors, lines, gratings, geometric figures, various objects or scenes, sounds) are represented in conscious perception in a nonveridical or distorted way. Most often encountered are visual, auditory, and tactile illusions. *Illusion* refers to incongruencies or distortions between perception and reality, to erroneous perception that emerges consistently and systematically under specific conditions of stimulation. (In practical use, illusions are regarded as being different from *hallucinations** and delusions. The object, the perception of which involves illusory experience, is itself real, objective, and actually present, whereas hallucinations do not have objective counterparts in an observer's current environment.)

The most common and well-known examples of illusions are the optical-geometric ones, where sizes, proportions, tilts, shapes, and so forth are misperceived or perceptually distorted. Such illusions are usually named either according to the names of the individuals who first discovered or described them or according to the essence of the illusory change involved. The list of the best-known and most thoroughly studied visual illusions includes the following: Müller-Lyer illusion (see Figure 26, left panel); Ponzo illusion; Poggendorf illusion; Zöllner illusion; Ebbinghaus size-contrast (see Figure 26, right panel); Fraser Spiral illusion; Oppel-Kundt illusion; Ladd-Franklin illusion; Sander parallelogram illusion; Orbison illusion; Wundt area illusion; Wundt bended lines illusion; Delboef illusion; Baldwin illusion; vertical-horizontal illusion; filled space illusion; rod and frame illusion. For instance, in the Müller-Lyer illusion, there are two lines of equal length situated between the arrowheads and the arrow tails; however, we perceive the line between the arrow tails as longer than the line between the arrowheads (compare left and right vertical shafts in Figure 26).

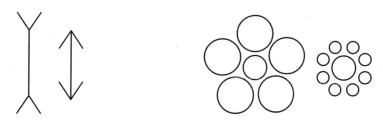

Figure 26

Many illusory experiences are *aftereffects,* such as in *figural afteref-fects** (see Figure 17), color aftereffects (see Figure 12); some of the on-line illusory experiences are generated with displays involving motion (*stroboscopic motion**, *induced motion**; see also *flash-lag effect**, *Fröhlich effect**); observing stimuli in motion also may create *motion aftereffects**. Some illusions are essentially constructive ones because instead of, or in addition to, distortions of the properties of the existing features and objects, new entities are formed in perception (e.g., *illusory contours**). Also, real features or characteristics of stimulation may become re-arranged in an illusory way (e.g., *illusory conjunctions**). Illusory experiences also may be a part of the *filling-in** phenomena.

Quite often, illusory experiences seem to be the result of cognitive processing that is internally biased as a result of long-term perceptual learning in that they tend to represent typical or most probable states of affairs in the sensory environment filled with various objects: the less likely characteristics and feature values, given the actual context of the items of stimulation, are substituted by more likely perceptual characteristics and feature values that, though illusory, happen to be most typical under the given circumstances. It is highly probable that higher level nodes in the processing system which most closely repre-sent typical, categorically specified, and generalized characteristics and properties send reentrant influences back to earlier processing levels that encode specific local features. Individuation of the sensory input in a unique and absolutely and precisely measured way is sacrificed in order to represent lawful and typical properties. In this back-propagation process, typicality-driven influences mold the pattern of activity of the local feature detectors in a way that creates more or less illusory yet highly expected experiences where the veridical blends with the imaginary (e.g., Bachmann, 1978, 1998; Hochstein & Ahissar, 2002; Rensink, 2000; Lamme, 2003). Conscious vision has the function of representing the best current interpretation of the environment (Crick & Koch, 2003). Interpretations are inevitably influenced by experience, and experience is inevitably biased toward the typical or more probable.

References

Bachmann, T. (1978). Cognitive contours: Overview and a preliminary theory. *Acta et Commentationes Universitatis Tartuensis: Problems of Communication and Perception, 474*, 31–59.

Bachmann, T. (1998). Filling-in as a within-level propagation may be an illusion. *Behavioral and Brain Sciences, 21*, 749–750.

Crick, F., & Koch, C. (2003). A framework for consciousness. *Nature Neuroscience, 6*, 119–126.

Dennett, D. (1991). *Consciousness explained.* Boston: Little & Brown.

Dennett, D. (2001). Are we explaining consciousness as yet? *Cognition, 79*, 221–237.

Deregowski, J. B. (1980). *Illusions, patterns and pictures.* London: Academic Press.

Ernst, B. (1992). *The eye beguiled: Optical illusions.* Berlin: Benedikt Taschen.

Gombrich, E. H. (1988). *Art and illusion.* London: Phaidon Press.

Gregory, R. L. (1970). *The intelligent eye.* London: Weidenfeld & Nicholson.

Gregory, R. L. (1978). *Eye and brain.* New York: McGraw-Hill.

Gregory, R. L. (1997). *Eye and brain: The psychology of seeing.* Princeton: Princeton University Press.

Hochstein, S., and Ahissar, M. (2002). View from the top: Hierarchies and reverse hierarchies in the visual system. *Neuron, 36*, 791–804.

Kanizsa, G. (1979). *Organization of vision: Essays on Gestalt perception.* New York: Praeger.

Lamme, V. A. F. (2003). Why visual attention and awareness are different. *Trends in Cognitive Sciences, 7*, 12–18.

Noë, A. (Ed.). (2002). *Is the visual world a grand illusion?* Thorverton, England: Imprint Academic.

Noë, A., Pessoa, L., & Thompson, E. (2000). Beyond the grand illusion: What change blindness really teaches us about vision. *Visual Cognition, 7*, 93–106.

O'Regan, J. K. (1992). Solving the 'real' mysteries of visual perception: The world as an outside memory. *Canadian Journal of Psychology, 46*, 461–488.

O'Regan, J. K. (2002). Vision: The grand illusion. In R. Carter (Ed.), *Consciousness* (pp. 16–17). London: Weidenfeld & Nicholson.

Rensink, R. A. (2000). Seeing, sensing, and scrutinizing. *Vision Research, 40*, 1469–1487.

Robinson, J. O. (1998). *The psychology of visual illusion.* London: Dover.

Rock, I. (1984). *Perception.* New York: Scientific American.

Seckel, A. (2000). *The art of optical illusions*. London: Carlton.
Seckel, A. (2002). *More optical illusions*. London: Carlton.

Illusory conjunctions

Objects typically have several features that characterize them. For instance, the blossom of a cowslip has its characteristic yellow color, size of leaves, orientation values of the contour which delineate the shape of the blossom, and a certain location in visual space. It is known that these features are encoded by sensory units in the brain which are located in different cortical areas. Yet in conscious perception, they belong to the same object, as if bound together. Understanding the process by which features processed in separate areas of the brain are combined into a unitary object-percept poses what in cognitive science is known as the *binding problem*. In some specific conditions, when attention is overloaded and there is a more or less demanding information processing task (especially if objects are presented for short times, and there are several objects competing for attention), illusory experiences may occur where features that actually belong to different (separate) objects become perceptually conjoined (integrated) in a nonveridical way as if belonging to the same object. The attributes of one object may be confused with the attributes of another object. Coren, Ward, and Enns (1994) define illusory conjunctions as a percept consisting of an incorrect integration of features from separate objects into a single perceptual object. Thus, a white Lexus car in motion in a gray city environment and a blue BMW car also present in the same crowded scene of traffic may provide conditions where perceptual experience of a blue Lexus emerges. In an experimental setting, while searching for a pre-specified target-object appearing in a larger, briefly presented display containing many other objects, it may happen that the observer sees, for instance, a red *T*, although only green *T*s and red *O*s are presented (Treisman & Schmidt, 1982).

Illusory conjunctions can be biased by former perceptual experience, expectancies, and cognitive sets. Feature misbinding can be strongly memory dependent. For example, Bruner and Postman (1949) showed to their observers a set of playing cards, asking them to report what card they saw. When experimentally incongruent cards were shown (e.g., a six of hearts, where hearts were depicted in black) observers often misperceived them according to the typical rules of color-shape conjunction (e.g., they "saw" a six of spades). In some cases, the color of a card symbol was a compromise between the actual and the expected (e.g., a red spade stimulus was perceived neither as red nor as black but as a symbol appearing in maroon). The latter result shows that binding should not necessarily work as a binary operation combining discrete values of the stimulus attributes but may work as an operation working on an analogue scale.

Importantly, illusory conjunctions are not constrained by the exact spatial properties and measures of the feature values involved: for instance, the color of a large object may be exchanged for the color of a smaller object and vice versa, so as to fit the constraints provided by the other feature with which it is integrated (see also the *Cai and Schlag effect**). This means that conscious experience of objects with multiple properties is a result of a higher level (or additional level) processing and not simply a summative (re)combinatorial operation.

References

Bruner, J. S., & Postman, L. (1949). On the perception of incongruity: A paradigm. *Journal of Personality, 18,* 206–223.

Coren, S., Ward, L. M., & Enns, J. T. (1994). *Sensation and Perception.* Fort Worth, TX: Harcourt Brace.

Revonsuo, A., & Newman, J. (1999). Binding and consciousness. *Consciousness and Cognition, 8,* 123–127.

Roskies, A. L. (1999). The binding problem. *Neuron, 24,* 7–9.

Treisman, A. (1986). Features and objects in visual processing. *Scientific American, 255,* 114–125.

Treisman, A. (1998). Feature binding, attention and object perception. *Philosophical Transactions of the Royal Society of London. Series B, Biological Sciences, 353,* 1295–1306.

Treisman, A., & Paterson, R. (1984). Emergent features, attention, and object perception. *Journal of Experimental Psychology: Human Perception and Performance, 10,* 12–21.

Treisman, A., & Schmidt, H. (1982). Illusory conjunctions in the perception of objects. *Cognitive Psychology, 14,* 107–141.

Illusory contours

In this special class of *illusions**, visual processing system creates visible contours or edges that are not actually a part of the physical display. Sometimes, illusory contours delineate or specify illusory objects, where only part of the object contour or edge is supported by physical luminance gradients and a big part (or even the majority) of the perceived object or figure is formed as an illusory experience. In Figure 27, left panel, the central large disk or ring is clearly perceived but represented in awareness mostly by illusory contour.

A large variety of illusory contours exist, and they have been given various names, such as anomalous contours; virtual contours; subjective contours; cognitive contours; quasi-perceptive margins; phantom lines; and so forth. The edges of illusory objects can be both apparently sharp or vague (or "hazy"). In addition, illusory surfaces and apparently transparent smoky plates can give rise to illusory objects. In the phenomenon of neon *color spreading**, the perceptual experience of a transparent object and colored filmy entity is formed. Illusory contour–based objects tend to have different (e.g., increased) subjective brightness compared to the brightness of an equiluminant background, and they often seem to be positioned at a closer depth plane, as if covering the part of the visual field which remains behind it or covering parts of the other objects. Incompleteness in figure or in the arrangement of the elements of the scene tends to foster emergence of illusory contours.

Illusory contours can mask real contours and create illusions, and the figures formed from illusory contours can be multistable, similar to the *reversible figures** containing real contours (as in the depth reversals of the faces of the cube shown Figure 27, right panel). Illusory contour perception is accompanied by the activity of the contour-sensitive neurons in the peristriate areas of the visual cortex. Perception of illusory contours develops microgenetically—it takes about 0.1–0.5 s after the exposure of the inducing stimuli until an illusory contour appears in awareness. Illusory contour–based form emerges in awareness even if the inducing real elements are rendered invisible by a mask. Illusory contour has longer visible persistence than real contours.

The theories for explaining the phenomena of illusory contours include cognitive inference (hypothesis testing), Gestalt organization,

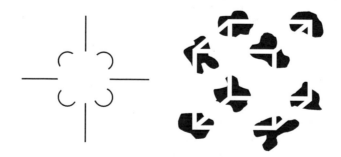

Figure 27

depth perception, long-range neural interactions in boundary formation, local visual contrast, and other factors that may be important in
the emergence of this spectacular illusion, where the contents of visual
awareness are not veridical. See also *amodal* and *modal completion**.

References

Bachmann, T. (1978). Cognitive contours: Overview and a preliminary theory.
    Acta et Commentationes Universitatis Tartuensis, 474, 31–59.
Coren, S. (1972). Subjective contours and apparent depth. *Psychological Review,*
    79, 359–367.
Ehrenstein, W. (1941). Über Abwandlungen der L. Hermannschen Helliskeit-
    serscheinung. *Zeitschrift für Psychologie, 150,* 83–91.
Frisby, J. P., & Clatworthy, J. L. (1975). Illusory contours: Curious cases of si-
    multaneous brightness contrast. *Perception, 4,* 349–357.
Gellatly, A. H. R. (1980). Perception of an illusory triangle with masked induc-
    ing figure. *Perception, 9,* 599–602.
Grossberg, S. & Mingolla, E. (1985). Neural dynamics of form perception:
    Boundary completion, illusory figures, and neon color spreading. *Psycholog-
    ical Review, 92,* 173–211.
Halpern, D. F. (1981). The determinants of illusory-contour perception. *Percep-
    tion, 10,* 191–213.
Kanizsa, G. (1955). Margini quasi-percettivi in campi con stimolazione omage-
    nea. *Rivista di Psicologia, 49,* 7–30.
Kanizsa, G. (1974). Contours without gradients or cognitive contours. *Italian
    Journal of Psychology, 1,* 93–112.
Kanizsa, G. (1976). Subjective contours. *Scientific American, 234,* 48–52.
Kanizsa, G. (1979). *Organization of vision: Essays on Gestalt perception.* New York:
    Praeger.
Kennedy, J. M. (1976). Sun figure: An illusory diffuse contour resulting from an
    arrangement of dots. *Perception, 5,* 475–481.
Parks, T. E. (1995). The microgenesis of illusory figures: Evidence for visual hy-
    pothesis testing. *Perception, 24,* 681–684.
Peterhans, E., & von der Heydt, R. (1991). Subjective contours: Bridging the gap
    between psychophysics and physiology. *Trends in Neurosciences, 14,* 112–119.
Petry, S., & Meyer, G. E. (Eds.). (1987). *The perception of illusory contours.* New
    York: Springer.
Ringach, D. L., & Shapley, R. (1996). Spatial and temporal properties of illusory
    contours and amodal boundary completion. *Vision Research, 36,*
    3037–3050.
Schumann, F. (1904). Einige beobachtungen über die Zusammenfassung von
    Gesichtseindrucken zu Einheiten. *Psychologische Studien, 1,* 1–23.
Takahashi, S. (1994). Microgenetic process of subjective contour perception in
    "noise-containing" inducing patterns. *Japanese Psychological Research, 36,*
    195–200.

van Tuijl, H. F. J. M. (1975). A new visual illusion: Neonlike color spreading and complementary color induction between subjective contours. *Acta Psychologica, 39,* 441–445.

von der Heydt, R., & Peterhans, E. (1989). Mechanisms of contour perception in monkey visual cortex. I. Lines of pattern discontinuity. *Journal of Neuroscience, 9,* 1731–1748.

von der Heydt, R., Peterhans, E., & Baumgartner, G. (1984). Illusory contours and cortical neuron responses. *Science, 224,* 1260–1262.

Induced-motion effects

When the visual field contains two visible objects (e.g., points of light) without any other visible spatial reference, and when one of the objects is stationary and the other is moving, either of the objects or both appear to move (e.g., Duncker, 1929). For the physically stationary object, this implies an illusion of *induced motion*. When a larger moving object encloses another smaller object, the smaller one appears to move relative to a stationary framework provided by the larger object. (See Figure 28: the solid arrow represents actual motion; the dashed arrow, illusory induced motion.) Induced motion for the embedded smaller object can be evoked also if the motion of the larger object remains below subjective motion threshold. With higher speeds of the actual motion of the inducing object, the subjectively induced motion of the stationary object becomes weaker. An experience of induced motion is often produced when a clearing in the clouds slowly drifting across the night sky exposes the stationary moon. Here, the moon often is (mis)perceived as moving relative to a stationary framework provided by the clouds.

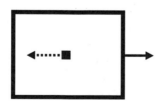

Figure 28

References

Day, R. H., & Dickinson, R. G. (1977). Absence of color selectivity in Duncker-type induced visual movement. *Perception and Psychophysics, 22,* 313–320.

Duncker, K. (1929). Über induzierte Bewegung. *Psychologische Forschung, 22,* 180–259.

Gogel, W. C., & Koslow, M. A. (1972). The adjacency principle and induced movement. *Psychonomic Science, 11,* 309–314.

Rock, I., Auster, M., Schiffman, H., & Wheeler, D. (1980). Induced movement based on the subtraction of motion from the inducing object. *Journal of Experimental Psychology: Human Perception and Performance, 6,* 391–403.

Wallach, H., Bacon, J., & Schulman, P. (1978). Alteration of induced motion. *Perception and Psychophysics, 24,* 509–514.

Inhibition of return

A physical attentional cue presented at a peripheral spatial location in the visual field facilitates target-object processing at that location for a postcue period of about 100 to 250 ms. This period of facilitation is followed at about 300 ms or more after the cue by a period in which target detection at that location is slowed down or impaired. The latter phenomenon is called *inhibition of return* (IOR). In the extreme cases of IOR, targets at that location, if presented after critical postcue delays, sometimes cannot be even consciously perceived. See also *covert spatial attention effect**.

References

Kingstone, A., & Pratt, J. (1999). Inhibition of return is composed of attentional and oculomotor processes. *Perception & Psychophysics, 61,* 1046–1054.

Posner, M. I., Rafal, R. D., Choate, L. S., & Vaughan, J. (1985). Inhibition of return: Neural basis and function. *Cognitive Neuropsychology, 2,* 211–228.

Inverted vision effects

When observers wear optical devices (e.g., mirrors or prisms) that invert the images from the environment projected onto retinas for a prolonged time (days or weeks) without allowing normal vision conditions, the visual world, which initially looked inverted, eventually appears to take on its normal upright orientation. Whether this is a genuine perceptual effect or just a flexible adaptation of visuomotor correlations to the new conditions of observation remains controversial. Nevertheless, observers regain the more or less normal capabilities of moving and navigating in the environment and manipulating objects. Subjectively, after a weeklong adaptation to the optical rearrangement by inverted vision, some common events with physically lawful components (pouring water, smoke rising from a cigarette) appear to occur in the normal direction in the apparently normally oriented, upright world. This indicates that the subjective visual world can be adapted to unusual optical conditions. The effect was first demonstrated and described by George Malcolm Stratton (1865–1957). After the removal of the prolonged visual inversion conditions, difficulties in readapting to normal viewing conditions are experienced for some time. See also *adaptation effects, prism adaptation effects**.

References

Kohler, I. (1962). Experiments with goggles. *Scientific American, 206*, 62–86.

Linden, D. E. I., Kallenbach, U., Heinecke, A., Singer, W., & Goebel, R. (1999). The myth of upright vision. A psychophysical and functional imaging study of adaptation to inverting spectacles. *Perception, 28*, 469–481.

Stratton, G. M. (1896). Some preliminary experiments on vision without inversion of the retinal image. *Psychological Review, 3*, 611–617.

Stratton, G. M. (1897). Upright vision and the retinal image. *Psychological Review, 4*, 182–187.

Stratton, G. M. (1897). Vision without inversion of the retinal image. *Psychological Review, 4*, 341–360.

Welch, R. B. (1978). *Perceptual modification, adapting to altered sensory environments*. New York: Academic Press.

Kravkov's effects

The Russian scientist Sergey Kravkov (1893–1951) demonstrated various effects of nonvisual stimulation on visual perception. For instance, an increase in the amount of adrenalin, ephedrine, or cordiamine augments an observer's sensitivity toward blue and green parts of the spectrum of visible light and decreases sensitivity to red and orange. Caffeine increases sensitivity to all spectral components. Exposure to a sound with an invariant frequency increases sensitivity to blue and green, while sensitivity to yellow remains unchanged. The effect of sound on blue-green luminance summation consists in decreasing the *critical flicker frequency (CFF)** for those wavelengths of light. However, CFF for light pulses in the red-orange part of the visible spectrum increases under the influence of a coherent sound. Similar effects on the CFF are exerted by certain smells, such as bergamot oil and geraniol. Rosemary increases the value of threshold perimeter for green stimuli and decreases the perimeter value for red. The taste of sugar increases sensitivity to green and decreases sensitivity to red. Also, sugar decreases CFF for green and increases CFF for red. Hyperventilation increases sensitivity to red and decreases sensitivity to green. See also *synesthesia**.

References

Kravkov, S. V. (1950). *Glaz i ego rabota* [*Eye and its performance*]. Moscow: Academy of Sciences Press.
Kravkov, S. V. (1955). *Das Farbsehen.* Berlin: Akademie.

Launching effect

See *phenomenal causality**.

Lawrence effect

When a rapid sequence (6–19 per s) of lowercase words appears at the same place in the visual field, and a target word written in uppercase letters is inserted into this stream, observers often report a wrong word as the target without even noticing that they made a mistake. In the majority of cases, the lowercase word erroneously perceived as the target follows the real target, but it rarely precedes it. The temporal positions from which the misattributed target words are sampled are close to the temporal position of the actual target. The effect was introduced by Lawrence (1971). See also substitution *masking**, *metacontrast, illusory conjunctions**.

Reference

Lawrence, D. H. (1971). Two studies of visual search for targets with controlled rates of presentation. *Perception and Psychophysics, 10,* 85–89.

Line-motion illusion

If a small visual object, such as a dot, is briefly flashed near one end of a following solid line, observers experience a dynamic illusion akin to *filling-in**: something in the line appears to grow or to move from the end of the line that is closest to the prior dot and to expand toward the other end of the line (e.g., see Hikosaka, Miyauchi, & Shimojo, 1993). The time intervals separating the prior dot from the line which optimize the illusion (sometimes called the *Hikosaka effect*) are in the range of 50 to 200 ms. The spatial extents of the optimal stimulus display range up to a few degrees of visual angle. The line-motion illusion can be modulated (even reversed) by proper spatial-attentional manipulations and by cuing with stimuli of a different modality (e.g., auditory cues). Also, the perceived direction of illusory line motion can be reversed by manipulating stimuli presented after the line disappears. This implies involvement of higher cognitive-level processes in generating this illusion. See also *covert spatial attention effect*, path-guided motion*, stroboscopic motion**.

References

Eagleman, D. M., & Sejnowski, T. J. (2003). The line-motion illusion can be reversed by motion signals after the line disappears. *Perception, 32,* 963–968.

Hikosaka, O., Miyauchi, S., & Shimojo, S. (1993). Voluntary and stimulus-induced attention detected as motion sensation. *Perception, 22,* 517–526.

Schmidt, W. C., Fisher, B. D., & Pylyshyn, Z. W. (1998). Multiple-location access in vision: Evidence from illusory line motion. *Journal of Experimental Psychology: Human Perception and Performance, 24,* 505–525.

Shimojo, S., Miyauchi, S., & Hikosaka, O. (1997). Visual motion sensation yielded by non-visually driven attention. *Vision Research, 37,* 1575–1580.

Masked object-priming

Despite the fact that the visibility (phenomenal presence) of a prime can be suppressed by an aftercoming, highly visible mask, the features of the prime, such as its color or form, can facilitate processing of, and discriminative responses to, similar features of the visible mask. Effects such as masked object-priming and *perceptual latency-priming** indicate that the visual system processes relatively many aspects of an object at a preconscious or unconscious level.

References

Breitmeyer, B. G., Öğmen, H., & Chen, J. (2004). Unconscious priming by color and form: Different processes and levels. *Consciousness and Cognition, 13,* 138–157.

Breitmeyer, B. G., Ro, T., & Singhal, N. (2004). Unconscious priming with chromatic stimuli occurs at stimulus- not percept-dependent levels of visual processing. *Psychological Science, 15,* 198–202.

Kinoshita, S. & Lupker, S. J. (2003). *Masked priming.* New York: Taylor & Francis.

Klotz, W., & Wolff, P. (1995). The effect of a masked stimulus on the response to the masking stimulus. *Psychological Research/Psychologische Forschung, 58,* 92–101.

Masking

A perceptual target stimulus, such as a line, letter, geometric form, grating, or picture, which can be perceived easily if presented in isolation becomes hard or impossible to perceive if another stimulus called the *mask* (or *masker*) is presented in the target's spatial and temporal proximity (or *neighborhood*). Typically, the sizes of masked targets and effective masks are in the range from a fraction of a degree of visual angle up to several degrees of visual angle. To be effective as a mask, the masking stimulus typically has to be at least as large as the target or larger. For a target stimulus to be masked, target durations and time intervals between target and mask have to be rather short. Typical durations of targets that can be effectively masked are from a few to a few tens of milliseconds; to obtain masking, the typical time intervals between a target and the mask should not exceed a maximum of 100–200 ms. The higher the intensity ratio between the mask and target (in favor of the mask), the stronger the masking. A situation close to masking occurs when objects presented briefly in only 1 frame (or 2–3 frames) of a cinematographic film, television broadcast, or a frame of a computer display for, say, 17 ms (or 34–50 ms) are followed by a completely different picture in the immediately following frames. This would render the objects invisible at a conscious level.

In *forward masking,* the mask is presented before the target. In *backward masking,* the mask is presented after the target. In *simultaneous masking,* target and mask are presented at the same time. Usually, backward-masking effects extend to longer time intervals than forward-masking effects; the following stimulus in time tends to dominate conscious perception (e.g., see Turvey, 1973; Bachmann & Allik, 1976; Michaels & Turvey, 1979). This can be termed as a replacement effect or *substitution masking.* Substitution masking typically occurs when the target and mask are well-articulated objects and when spatial attention is not narrowly focused on the target location before its exposure. The most spectacular substitution masking is obtained when a brief target stimulus (e.g., a Landolt C with a gap in 1 of 4 possible locations—up, right, down, or left) located among several equally brief distractor stimuli is spatially surrounded by, say, a masking ring whose onset is simultaneous with that of the target but whose offset is delayed by several tens of milliseconds after the offset of the target. (Often, these are called *simultaneous onset, asynchronous offset,* displays.) When spatial attention of the observer is directed to the target location before its presentation, substitution masking fails to occur. However, when spatial attention is not focused at the target location, observers fail to see the target and see the mask instead. Substitution masking in the conditions of nonfocused spatial attention also can be caused by a so-called *weak mask* (e.g., 4 small dots surrounding the target-object) which in ordinary masking conditions is unable to have any strong masking effect. (For a thorough overview of substitution-masking effects and theory, see Enns & DiLollo, 1997, 2000; DiLollo, Enns, & Rensink, 2000.)

In addition to masks that are articulated objects, masking effects also can be produced by uniform flashes of light, random patterns, and noise. A special case of masking is called *metacontrast*. In metacontrast, a target-object (a bar, a disk, a diamond, etc.) is followed by a mask that does not spatially overlap with the target but is presented in an immediately adjacent or very close spatial location. Metacontrast is strong when the mask structure (defined by its contours, edges) flanks or surrounds (*embraces*) the target-object. In a classic paper by Werner (1935), the target disk when followed by a masking ring that tightly surrounds it becomes nearly or totally invisible if the time interval between the onset of the target disk (e.g., presented for 10 ms) and the onset of the masking ring is about 40–80 ms. Metacontrast masking is negligible or absent when target and mask onsets are simultaneous or nearly so (e.g., onset asynchronies of 5–20 ms), as well as when the onsets are separated by larger intervals (e.g., 150–200 ms). This creates the so-called *U-shaped or nonmonotonic (Type-B) functions of masking*, where masking is weak or absent at very short and at longer time intervals but strong or severe at intermediate time intervals between target and mask. Surprisingly, metacontrast tends to be somewhat weaker (Breitmeyer, 1978) or even to disappear (Becker & Anstis, 2004) when target and mask are presented on a gray background as opposite-polarity contrast stimuli—for example, a mask depicted as white on gray and a target as black on gray, or vice versa. Sometimes, *between-object (mutual) masking* in the case of spatially overlapping targets also yields a U-shaped masking function for the first target (e.g., Bachmann & Allik, 1976; Michaels & Turvey, 1979).

While metacontrast tends to generate nonmonotonic (U-shaped or J-shaped) variations of target visibility as a function of *stimulus onset asynchrony* (SOA) between target and mask, masking by light or noise tends to generate monotonic masking functions. In the latter case, the longer the time interval between target and mask, the weaker the masking is.

The fact that a masked target is invisible (out of conscious awareness) does not mean that it is not visually or cognitively processed. There are numerous findings showing that masked stimuli not registering in consciousness (i.e., psychologically not explicit) nevertheless are processed in terms of their visual, semantic, emotional, and other characteristics and properties by preconscious brain processes. This can lead to *perceptual latency-priming** for a backward mask even when the target's visibility is completely suppressed. It also leads to a variety of masked priming effects: for instance, to semantic priming by the effectively masked semantic stimuli, to perceptual priming, to priming of numerical tasks, and to affective priming of some evaluative or psychophysiological automatic reactions (de Gelder, de Haan, & Heywood, 2001; Dehaene & Naccache, 2001; Kinoshita & Lupker, 2003; Marcel, 1983; Morris, Öhman, & Dolan, 1998; Naccache & Dehaene, 2001; Naccache, Blandin, & Dehaene, 2002). Modern brain imaging methods have allowed observations of cortical (e.g., occipital, inferotemporal, prefrontal) and subcortical (e.g., amygdala-related) activities that correlate with preconscious processing of masked stimulation.

For effective masking to occur, target and mask also may be presented in repetitive cycles, so that target exposures and mask exposures are intermittent, alternating (Werner, 1935). In one such effect, called the *standing wave of invisibility* illusion, a repetitively metacontrast-masked stimulus can remain invisible for quite a long time with only the mask stimulus registering in awareness (e.g., Werner, 1935; Macknik & Livingstone, 1998; Macknik, Martinez-Conde, & Haglund, 2000; Enns, 2002). Importantly, even though the target is invisible, its visual properties and characteristics influence the visual appearance of the visible mask. This is similar to the *feature inheritance** phenomenon.

In essence, masking appears to be a procedure where the mask presentation prevents target information from reaching a state of stable conscious representation; however, this occurs without eliminating the high-level preconscious processing of the target's characteristics and properties (Bachmann, 1984; Price, 2001).

Seminal studies of visual masking have been carried out by Baxt (1871), Stigler (1910), Baade (1917), Werner (1935), Piéron (1925, 1935), Crawford (1947), Alpern (1953), Schiller and Chorover (1966), and Kinsbourne and Warrington (1962), among many others. For reviews of masking, see Kahneman (1968), Breitmeyer (1984), Bachmann (1994), Breitmeyer and Öğmen (2000, 2006), and Francis (2000).

Various kinds of masking functions also can be obtained in other modalities like hearing and touch, including monotonic as well as non-monotonic, U- and J-shaped (metacontrast) functions (Berlin, Lowell-Bell, Cullen, Thompson, & Loovis, 1973, Berlin, Berlin, Hughes, & Dermody, 1976; Craig, 1995; Craig & Xiuying, 1997; Studdert-Kennedy, Shankweiler, & Schulman, 1970).

References

Alpern, M. (1953). Metacontrast. *Journal of the Optical Society of America, 43,* 648–657.

Baade, W. (1917). Experimentelle Untersuchungen zur darstellenden Psychologie des Wahrnehmungsprozesses. *Zeitschrift für Psychologie und Physiologie der Sinnesorgane, 79,* 97–127.

Bachmann, T. (1984). The process of perceptual retouch: Nonspecific afferent activation dynamics in explaining visual masking. *Perception and Psychophysics, 35,* 69–84.

Bachmann, T. (1994). *Psychophysiology of visual masking: The fine structure of conscious experience.* Commack, NY: Nova Science.

Bachmann, T., & Allik, J. (1976). Integration and interruption in the masking of form by form. *Perception, 5,* 79–97.

Baxt, N. (1871). Über die Zeit, welche nötig ist, damit ein Gesichtseindruck zum Bewusstein kommt und über die Grösse (Extension) der bewussten Wahrnehmung bei einem Gesichtseindrucke von gegebener Dauer. *Pflügers Archiv für Gesamte Physiologie der Menschen und Tiere, 4,* 325–336.

Becker, M. W., & Anstis, S. (2004). Metacontrast masking is specific to luminance polarity. *Vision Research, 44,* 2537–2543.

Berlin, C. I., Berlin, H. L., Hughes, L. F., & Dermody, P. (1976). Dichotic vs. monotic masking functions may reveal central organization for speech identification. *Journal of the Acoustical Society of America, 59,* 55.

Berlin, C. I., Lowell-Bell, S. S., Cullen, J. K., Jr., Thompson, C. L., & Loovis, C. F. (1973). Dichotic speech perception: An interpretation of right-ear advantage and temporal offset effects. *Journal of the Acoustical Society of America, 53,* 699–709.

Breitmeyer, B. G. (1978). Metacontrast with black and white stimuli: Evidence for inhibition of *on* and *off* sustained activity by either *on* or *off* transient activity. *Vision Research, 18,* 1443–1448.

Breitmeyer, B. G. (1984). *Visual masking: An integrative approach.* Oxford: Clarendon.

Breitmeyer, B. G., & Öğmen, H. (2000). Recent models and findings in backward masking: A comparison, review and update. *Perception and Psychophysics, 62,* 1572–1595.

Breitmeyer, B. G., & Öğmen, H. (2006). *Visual masking: Time slices through conscious and unconscious vision.* New York: Oxford University Press.

Craig, J. C. (1995). Vibrotactile masking: The role of response competition. *Perception and Psychophysics, 57,* 1190–1200.

Craig, J. C., & Xiuying, Q. (1997). Tactile pattern perception by two fingers: Temporal interference and response competition. *Perception and Psychophysics, 59,* 252–265.

Crawford, B. H. (1947). Visual adaptation in relation to brief conditioning stimuli. *Proceedings of the Royal Society of London. Series B, Biological Sciences, 134,* 283–302.

de Gelder, B., de Haan, E., & Heywood, C. (Eds.). (2001). *Out of mind: Varieties of unconscious processes*. Oxford: Oxford University Press.

Dehaene, S., & Naccache, L. (2001). Towards a cognitive neuroscience of consciousness: Basic evidence and a workspace framework. *Cognition, 79,* 1–37.

DiLollo, V., Enns, J. T., & Rensink, R. A. (2000). Competition for consciousness among visual events: The psychophysics of reentrant visual processes. *Journal of Experimental Psychology: General, 129,* 481–507.

Enns, J. T. (2002). Visual binding in the standing wave illusion. *Psychonomic Bulletin and Review, 9,* 489–496.

Enns, J. T., & DiLollo, V. (1997). Object substitution: A new form of masking in unattended visual locations. *Psychological Science, 8,* 135–139.

Enns, J. T., & DiLollo, V. (2000). What's new in visual masking? *Trends in Cognitive Sciences, 4,* 345–352.

Francis, G. (2000). Quantitative theories of metacontrast masking. *Psychological Review, 107,* 768–785.

Kahneman, D. (1968). Method, findings, and theory in studies of visual masking. *Psychological Bulletin, 70,* 404–425.

Kinoshita, S., & Lupker, S. J. (Eds.). (2003). *Masked priming: The state of the art.* New York: Psychology.

Kinsbourne, M., & Warrington, E. K. (1962). The effect of an after-coming random pattern on the perception of brief visual stimuli. *Quarterly Journal of Experimental Psychology, 14,* 223–234.

Macknik, S. L., & Livingstone, M. S. (1998). Neuronal correlates of visibility and invisibility in the primate visual system. *Nature Neuroscience, 1,* 144–149.

Macknick, S. L., Martinez-Conde, S., & Haglund, M. M. (2000). The role of spatiotemporal edges in visibility and visual masking. *Proceedings of the National Academy of Sciences USA, 97,* 7556–7560.

Marcel, A. J. (1983). Conscious and unconscious perception: Experiments on visual masking and word recognition. *Cognitive Psychology, 15,* 197–237.

Michaels, C. F., & Turvey, M. T. (1979). Central sources of visual masking: Indexing structures supporting seeing at a single, brief glance. *Psychological Research, 41,* 1–61.

Morris, J. S., Öhman, A., & Dolan, R. J. (1998). Conscious and unconscious emotional learning in the human amygdala. *Nature, 393,* 467–470.

Naccache, L., Blandin, E., & Dehaene, S. (2002). Unconscious masked priming depends on temporal attention. *Psychological Science, 13,* 416–424.

Naccache, L., & Dehaene, S. (2001). The priming method: Imaging unconscious repetition priming reveals an abstract representation of number in parietal lobes. *Cerebral Cortex, 11,* 966–974.

Piéron, H. (1925). Recherches experimentales sur la marge de variation du temps de latence de la sensation lumineuse (par une méthode de masquage). *L'Année Psychologique, 26,* 1–30.

Piéron, H. (1935). Le processus du métacontraste. *Journal de Psychologie Normale et Pathologique, 32,* 5–24.

Price, M. (2001). Now you see it, now you don't: Preventing consciousness with visual masking. In P. Grossenbacher (Ed.), *Consciousness in the brain: A neurocognitive approach (Advances in Consciousness Research, 8)* (pp. 25–60). Amsterdam: John Benjamins.

Schiller, P. H., & Chorover, S. L. (1966). Metacontrast: Its relation to evoked potentials. *Science, 153,* 1398–1400.

Stigler, R. (1910). Chronophotische Studien über den Umgebungskontrast. *Pflügers Archiv der Gesamte Physiologie, 135,* 365–435.

Studdert-Kennedy, M., Shankweiler, D., & Schulman, S. (1970). Opposed effects of a delayed channel on perception of dichotically and monotically presented CV syllables. *Journal of the Acoustical Society of America, 48,* 599–602.

Turvey, M. T. (1973). On peripheral and central processes in vision: Inferences from an information-processing analysis of masking with patterned stimuli. *Psychological Review, 80,* 1–52.

Werner, H. (1935). Studies on contour: I. Qualitative analyses. *American Journal of Psychology, 47,* 40–64.

McCollough effect

This effect belongs to the family of *contingent aftereffects* and represents the most famous of them (McCollough, 1965). In the McCollough effect, the perceived color of a test grating depends on the orientation of that test grating when it is presented after two sequentially alternating conditioning (or adaptation) gratings, of which one is horizontal and the other is vertical. For example, a vertical grating consisting of black and orange bars is presented for 10 s and then replaced by a horizontal grating consisting of black and blue bars which is presented for 10 s. This sequence is repeated for about 10 min. After this induction (or inspection, or adaptation) period, a test grating consisting of black and white bars is presented. Observers shown the test gratings report seeing an illusory color that (a) is contingent on the orientation of the test grating and (b) appears as the complementary color of the conditioning grating; specifically, the vertical test grating appears to be blue, while the horizontal test grating appears orange. Hence, in this illusion, the color of the afterimage is not determined only by the color of the inspection (or conditioning) image (see Figure 12) but also by the orientation of the image's constituent features. Surprisingly, the McCollough effect can persist for hours and even many weeks, provided that no other conditioning and test procedures intervene. An effect almost identical to the McCollough effect can be produced even when observers imagine the inducing stimuli. The effect refers to selective binding between features and indirectly supports constructivist accounts of conscious perception demonstrating the flexibility in combining different features, such as color and orientation, to form coherent, multifeatured objects (á la Irvin Rock, Richard Gregory, William Epstein, Anne Treisman). Discovered and first described by Celeste Faye McCollough (b. 1926). Contingent aftereffects can be established between many other pairs of stimulus dimensions: for example, color and motion, color and depth, depth and motion, color and spatial frequency, form (or texture) and motion, faces and motion, and so forth See also *aftereffects**, *illusory conjunctions**, *selective adaptation.*

References

Anstis, S. M., & Harris, J. P. (1975). Movement aftereffects contingent on binocular disparity. *Perception, 3,* 153–168.

Breitmeyer, B. G., & Cooper, L. (1972). Frequency-specific color adaptation in the human visual system. *Perception and Psychophysics, 11,* 95–96.

Domini, F., Blaser, E., & Cicerone, C. (2000) Color-specific depth mechanisms revealed by a color-contingent depth aftereffect. *Vision Research, 40,* 359–364.

Fang, F., & He, S. (2002). Face-contingent motion aftereffect. *Journal of Vision, 2,* 616a.

Finke, R. A., & Schmidt, M. J. (1977). Orientation-specific color aftereffects following imagination. *Journal of Experimental Psychology: Human Perception and Performance, 3,* 599–606.

Harris, J. P. (1987). Contingent perceptual aftereffect. In R. L. Gregory (Ed.), *The Oxford companion to the mind* (pp. 166–168). Oxford: Oxford University Press.

Jenkins, B., & Ross, J. (1977). McCollough effect depends on perceptual organization. *Perception, 6,* 399–400.

Mayhew, J. E. W., & Anstis, S. M. (1972). Motion aftereffects contingent on color, intensity and pattern. *Perception and Psychophysics, 12,* 77–85.

McCollough, C. (1965). Color adaptation of edge-detectors in the human visual system. *Science, 149,* 1115–1116.

Skowbo, D., Timney, B. N., Gentry, T. A., & Morant, R. B. (1975). McCollough effects: Experimental findings and theoretical accounts. *Psychological Bulletin, 82,* 497–510.

Thompson, P. G., & Movshon, J. A. (1978). Storage of spatially specific threshold elevation. *Perception, 7,* 65–73.

McGurk effect

Speech perception is not restricted to the auditory modality. In suitable conditions, stimuli in visual or other modalities can modulate auditory perception. One of the most spectacular illusions or effects in the family

of intermodal effects was discovered by Harry McGurk and John Mac-
Donald (McGurk & MacDonald, 1976) and belongs to the domain of
audiovisual speech perception: illusory auditory perception is produced
if the visual information from lip movements is discrepant from the auditory information from the voice. When a face of a model who is ut-
tering certain syllables is videotaped, and when afterward the audible
part of the recording is replaced by audible sounds of the syllables different from those uttered by the visible model, perceivers may experience illusory sounds, so that the misperceived auditory syllable is not a
syllable or phoneme actually presented in the auditory modality, nor is
the visible syllable an actual "viseme" in the video part of the display.
With some syllabic visual-auditory recombinations, the illusion is hard
to produce; with some other combinations, the McGurk effect is robust.
For instance, when the visual /ga/ (in a repeated utterance "ga-ga") is
presented in synchrony with the auditory /ba/ (in a repeated utterance
"ba-ba"), observers hear an illusory fusion "da-da." Closing of the eyes
is sufficient to hear the correct "ba-ba" and to understand that the auditory perception was distorted. It is interesting to note that the effect is
quite robust in terms of its tendency to persist, even when the image of
the speaker's face is spatially quantized so that the mouth area is depicted only by about 4×2 square-shaped pixels. In addition to strictly
the mouth area, other surrounding areas of the speaker's face, such as
the jaw, can also modulate the McGurk effect somewhat.

Another example of a spectacular cross-modal interaction between
sight and sound is the so-called *ventriloquist effect* (e.g., Bertelson, 1998).
If synchronous auditory and visual stimuli are presented from slightly
separate locations, the perceived location of the sound is misplaced in
the direction of the visual object. In everyday circumstances, this effect
occurs when we perceive the source of the sound that a singer or
speaker produces on a television screen not from where the loudspeak-
ers are located but as if originating from where the image of the per-
former is. (The opposite bias—visual location misplaced toward the auditory stimulus—is weaker and rare.) See also *illusions*, synesthesia*,
sound-induced illusory flash*, Galli effect*.*

References

Bertelson, P. (1998). Starting from the ventriloquist: The perception of multi-
   modal events. In M. Sabourin, F. I. M. Craik, & M. Robert (Eds.), *Advances in
   psychological science, II: Biological and cognitive aspects* (pp. 419–439). Hove,
   England: Psychology Press.

Campbell, C. S., & Massaro, D. W. (1997). Perception of visible speech: Influence of spatial quantization. *Perception, 26,* 627–644.

MacDonald, J., Andersen, S., & Bachmann, T. (2000). Hearing by eye: How much spatial degradation can be tolerated? *Perception, 29,* 1155–1168.

MacDonald, J., & McGurk, H. (1978). Visual influences on speech perception processes. *Perception and Psychophysics, 24,* 253–257.

Massaro, D. W. (1998). *Perceiving talking faces: From speech perception to a behavioral principle.* Cambridge, MA: Bradford/MIT Press.

Massaro, D. W., & Cohen, M. M. (1995). Perceiving talking faces. *Current Directions in Psychological Science, 4,* 104–109.

McGurk, H., & MacDonald, J. (1976). Hearing lips and seeing voices. *Nature, 264,* 746–748.

Munhall, K. G., Gribble, P., Sacco, L., & Ward, M. (1996). Temporal constraints on the McGurk effect. *Perception and Psychophysics, 58,* 351–362.

Summerfield, A. Q. (1992). Lipreading and audio-visual speech perception. *Philosophical Transactions of the Royal Society of London. Series B, Biological Sciences, 335,* 71–78.

Vroomen, J., Bertelson, P., & de Gelder, B. (2001). Auditory-visual spatial interaction: Automatic versus intentional components. In B. de Gelder, E. H. F. de Haan, C. A. Heywood (Eds.), *Out of mind: Varieties of unconscious processes* (pp. 140–150). Oxford: Oxford University Press.

Walker, S., Bruce, V., & O'Malley, C. (1995). Facial identity and facial speech processing: Familiar faces and voices in the McGurk effect. *Perception and Psychophysics, 57,* 1124–1133.

Metacontrast

See *masking*.

Michotte effect

See *phenomenal causality*.

Modal completion

In *modal completion,* an unstimulated part of the visual field is filled in by the perceptual content that has a clearly experienced sensory content in it. *Illusory contours* comprise examples of modal completion. Other examples are perceptual *filling-in* phenomena. While observing a visual field containing a texture, observers perceive the continuation of a texture even where its image is projected on the blind spot in the retina. The blind spot is the small area in the retina where the fibers comprising the optic nerve exit the retina and where sensory receptors (rods and cones) are absent. Phenomena superficially similar to modal completion can emerge also in *visual masking** and in *binocular rivalry**: for example, if one eye is stimulated by a large white disk for a brief instant, and if a small white square on a black background is presented to the other eye for a brief instant and about 0.05 s later than the large disk, observers experience the small white square surrounded by a narrow area of black background which in a graded fashion spreads into the white area of the large white disk. The small square seems to have a darker halo around it (see *halo effect** and the accompanying Figure 24), which in turn is surrounded by the light area of the large disc. The spatial border between the halo and the surface of the larger white area is hazy and indistinct, with a gradient of brightness growing from bright close to the square to the darker shade closer to the fully visible regions of the large gray square.

References

See references for *filling-in**, *halo effect**, *amodal completion**, *illusory contours**.

Paradiso, M. A., & Nakayama, K (1991). Brightness perception and filling in. *Vision Research, 31,* 1221–1236.

Stoper, A. E., & Mansfield, J. G. (1978). Metacontrast and paracontrast suppression of a contourless area. *Vision Research, 18,* 1669–1674.

Motion aftereffect

A specific *aftereffect** produced by adapting to a moving display for a period of time, usually on the order of 30 s, and then looking at a stationary display. The stationary display appears to move in a direction opposite that of the adapting motion. Aristotle reported a version of this effect after looking at a waterfall for a while and then looking at the rocks next to the waterfall. The rocks appeared to drift upward, in a direction opposite to the falling water. For that reason, the effect is sometimes also called the *waterfall illusion.* Similar to *figural aftereffects**, motion aftereffects in humans are thought to result from adapting cortical detectors; in this case, from adapting directionally selective motion detectors. A common way to experience the motion aftereffect is to observe the landscape passing by behind the window of a moving train or coach and then noticing the apparent reverse motion of the environmental layout when the vehicle has just stopped. See also *aftereffect, illusion**, selective adaptation.*

References

Barlow, H. B., & Brindley, G. S. (1963). Intraocular transfer of movement after-effects during pressure blinding of the stimulated eye. *Nature, 200,* 1347.

Barlow, H. B., & Hill, R. M. (1963). Evidence for a physiological explanation of the waterfall illusion and figural after-effects. *Nature, 200,* 1345–1347.

Sekuler, R. W., & Ganz, L. (1963). After-effect of seen motion with a stabilized image. *Science, 139,* 419–420.

Motion capture

The ability of one stimulus to transfer aspects of its motion to another stimulus, thus capturing it into its motion regime. For example, an incoherently moving array of random dots, in which each dot moves in a random direction from frame to frame (resembling *Brownian motion*), appears to move coherently in the direction of a drifting sinusoidally modulated spatial grating. Motion of objects defined not only by luminance contrast but also by color contrast and by illusory contours can capture motion. Typically, the motion of larger or low spatial-frequency patterns captures the motion of small or high spatial-frequency patterns, although this depends on parameters like the magnitude of the luminance or color-contrast of the coherently moving stimuli.

References

Culham, J. C., & Cavanagh, P. (1994). Motion capture of luminance stimuli by equiluminous color gratings and by attentive tracking. *Vision Research, 34,* 2701–2706.

Ramachandran, V. S. (1986). Capture of stereopsis and apparent motion by illusory contours. *Perception and Psychophysics, 39,* 361–373.

Ramachandran, V. S., & Anstis, S. M. (1986). The perception of apparent motion. *Scientific American, 254,* 102–109.

Ramanchandran, V. S., & Cavanagh, P. (1987). Motion capture anisotropy. *Vision Research, 27,* 97–106.

Motion-induced blindness

When few clearly distinguishable stationary visual objects (e.g., yellow disks) are located within a set of numerous, coherently moving small random dots (e.g., tiny blue light sources moving around on a dark background), observers quite soon experience the sense that some or all of the stationary objects disappear from awareness (from visual experience). The spatial loci of the stationary objects appear as empty regions of the background. After disappearance, the target-objects begin to reappear in awareness in an apparently random manner, and then they may disappear again. The periods of target invisibility extend up to many seconds. If the same inducer-dots are stationary, perceptual loss of visual experience for the target-objects rarely happens. In typical motion-induced blindness displays, the stationary target-objects have a small region of empty space surrounding them where moving dots do not appear (*protective zones*). Thus, the effect cannot be reduced to merely some form of local spatial inhibition. Eye movements tend to restore quickly conscious visibility of the targets. Low-contrast target images tend to disappear more easily than high-contrast targets. The phenomenon was introduced by Bonneh, Cooperman, and Sagi (2001). Importantly, functional blindness involved temporarily in the motion-induced blindness effect does not mean that sensory processing of the objects is terminated or stopped while they are out of consciousness; when the currently suppressed object changes during its suppression phase, it reenters consciousness with the feature value that corresponds to the new, changed value and not the old value that it had at the moment when it did fade out of awareness (e.g., see Mitroff and Scholl, 2005). See also *fading effects*, multistability*, filling-in*, Ganzfeld**.

References

Bonneh, Y. S., Cooperman, A., & Sagi, D. (2001). Motion-induced blindness in normal observers. *Nature, 411,* 798–801.

Graf, E. W., Adams, W. J., & Lages, M. (2002). Modulating motion-induced blindness with depth ordering and surface completion. *Vision Research, 42,* 2731–2735.

Hofstoetter, C., Koch, C., & Kiper, D. C. (2004). Motion-induced blindness does not affect the formation of negative afterimages. *Consciousness and Cognition, 13,* 691–708.

Hsu, L.-C., Yeh, S.-L., & Kramer, P. (2004). Linking motion-induced blindness to perceptual filling-in. *Vision Research, 44,* 2857–2866.

Mitroff, S. R., & Scholl, B. J. (2005). Forming and updating object representations without awareness: Evidence from motion-induced blindness. *Vision Research, 45,* 961–967.

Motion-induced color mixture effect

A stationary, vertical, red-green square-wave grating is viewed through an array of vertical slits such that only one cycle of the grating is visible behind each slit. The slit-array moves horizontally by discrete steps equal to the half period of the grating. When the time interval between horizontal steps of the array is long, an observer perceives a veridical red-green grating. However, when this time interval is less than approximately 12 ms, the observer perceives yellow bars, even though red and green are not simultaneously present at any retinotopic location.

Reference

Nishida, S., Watanabe, J., Tachi, S., & Kuriki, I. (2004). Motion-induced color mixture. *Journal of Vision, 4,* 162a.

Moving phantoms

See perceptual *filling-in**, *amodal completion**.

Multiple flash effects

When a brief flash follows the offset of a long-duration light field, observers perceive this flash veridically as a single flash, provided that the time interval between the offset of the light field and the onset of the flash is either short (less than 100 ms) or long (more than 300 ms). However, for intermediate inter-stimulus intervals (ISIs), the single flash is perceived as a double flash.

When two brief flashes (5–10 ms) are presented superimposed at the same spatial location, observers can perceive 1, 2, and 3 or more flashes, depending on the ISI. For short ISIs (less than 50 ms), the perception of a single flash dominates. For long ISIs (more than 180 ms), the veridical perception of two flashes dominates. For ISIs between 50 and 180 ms, observers report seeing 3 or more flashes in a substantial number of trials. This phenomenon occurs for suprathreshold flashes, one or more log units above their detection threshold.

References

Bowen, R. W., (1989). Two pulses seen as three flashes: A superposition analysis. *Vision Research, 4,* 409–417.

Bowen, R. W., Mallow, J., & Harder, P. J. (1987). Some properties of the double flash illusion. *Journal of the Optical Society of America, 4,* 746–755.

Bowen, R. W., Markell, K. A., & Schoon, C. S. (1980). Two pulse discrimination and rapid light adaptation: Complex effects on temporal resolution and a new visual temporal illusion. *Journal of the Optical Society of America, 70,* 1453–1458.

Purushothaman, G., Öğmen, H., & Bedell, H. E. (2003). Suprathreshold intrinsic dynamics of the human visual system. *Neural Computation, 15,* 2883–2908.

Multistability

In certain special stimulation conditions, such as those showing *ambiguous figures**, reversible figure-ground stimuli, moving plaid patterns, or when *binocular rivalry** prevails or an ambiguous *stroboscopic motion** display is presented, the invariant physical stimulation permits variation in the ways that this stimulation is perceived. There are more than one state of perceptual stability that alternate in turns: for example, the same drawing of a figure can be perceptually interpreted and experienced as either a duck or a rabbit; when two mutually discrepant pictures are each presented to a different eye, only one can be consciously perceived at a time, sooner or later being replaced by the other alternative, which for a while itself will be represented in awareness in a stable form, only to be substituted by the initial alternative again, and so on. A moving plaid pattern composed of two overlapping orthogonal gratings can be seen alternately as a coherently moving plaid or two gratings drifting over and past each other. In Figure 29, a set of triangles is seen and perceived as a group pointing to 1 of the 3 possible directions; after some time, the direction that the triangles are pointing at suddenly changes, and the new version of the directional preference dominates awareness for some time, and so forth.

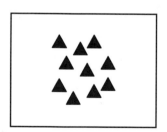

Figure 29

Negative afterimage

As another type of *complementary afterimage**, negative afterimage emerges as a light image if the adapting image had been dark, and it emerges as a dark image if the adapting image had been light. Similarly, in the successive *color contrast**, prolonged observation of an adapting stimulus with certain color induces an afterimage that has a complementary color to the adapting stimulus. Negative afterimage refers to achromatic aspect of afterimages contrary to the chromatic aspects involved in successive *color contrast**. See also *afterimage, contrast*, successive contrast.*

Neon color spreading

See *color spreading*, illusory contours*, filling-in*.*

Order reversal effect

See *temporal order reversal effect*.*

Path-guided motion

When a third object is inserted between the two stroboscopic stimuli that are flashed in succession, the path of apparent movement from the first to the second stimulus may be influenced by the form and shape of the third, intervening object: observers experience the sensation of motion between the two stimuli as if something moves along the trajectory that is defined by the third object. One possible way of arranging the stimuli for path-guided motion is depicted in Figure 30. A good path-guided motion effect can be obtained when a gray path is used. Path objects that include lines along the motion trajectory allow stronger motion effects to be experienced than paths including elements orthogonal to the direction of motion or elements that are spatially interrupted. The minimum time interval between the successive stimuli which still yields apparent motion increases not with the direct distance between the stroboscopic stimuli but linearly, with the length of the indirect path. Neural and motor responses to path-guided motion are in

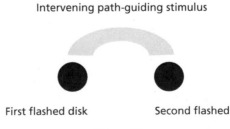

Intervening path-guiding stimulus

First flashed disk   Second flashed

Figure 30

many respects similar to the neural and motor responses to the real motion along the path delineated by the path-guided motion display elements. Also, path-guided motion stimulation is capable of decreasing the masking effect of the apparent-motion process if the path guides the apparent motion away from the spatial location of the target stimuli. See also *stroboscopic motion*, line motion illusion**.

References

Francis, G., & Kim, H. (1999). Motion parallel to line orientation: Disambiguation of motion percepts. *Perception, 28,* 1243–1255.

Merchant, H., Battaglia-Mayer, A., & Georgopoulos, A. P. (2004). Neural responses in motor cortex and area 7a to real and apparent motion. *Experimental Brain Research, 154,* 291–307.

Port, N. L., Pellizzer, G., & Georgopoulos, A. P. (1996). Intercepting real and path-guided apparent motion targets. *Experimental Brain Research, 110,* 298–307.

Shepard, R. N., & Zare, S. L. (1983). Path-guided apparent motion. *Science, 220,* 632–634.

Yantis, S., & Nakama, T. (1998). Visual interactions in the path of apparent motion. *Nature Neuroscience, 1,* 508–512.

Perceptual asynchrony effect

When two different features of an object change simultaneously, observers may perceive these feature changes as temporally asynchronous. For example, when the color and motion-direction of an array of dots change periodically and observers are asked to report the predominant color during the time intervals when the dots move in a specific direction (e.g., upward), the physical phase of directional change has to shift approximately 80 ms with respect to the physical phase of color change for these features to appear perceptually in phase. However, if observers are asked to judge the temporal order of color versus motion change, the illusion vanishes. Thus the nature of criterion content is critical in observing the perceptual asynchrony effects. See also *illusory conjunctions*, Cai and Schlag effect*, flash-lag effect**.

References

Arnold, D. H., Clifford, C. W., & Wenderoth, P. (2001). Asynchronous processing in vision: Color leads motion. *Current Biology, 11,* 596–600.

Bedell, H. E., Chung, S. T. L., Öğmen, H., & Patel, S. S. (2003). Color and motion: Which is the tortoise and which is the hare? *Vision Research, 43,* 2403–2412.

Llinares, L., & López-Molinar, J. (2006). Perceptual asynchrony between color and motion with a single direction change. *Journal of Vision, 6,* 974–981.

Moutoussis, K., & Zeki, S. (1997). A direct demonstration of perceptual asynchrony in vision. *Proceedings of the Royal Society of London. Series B, Biological Sciences, 264,* 393–399.

Nishida, S., Johnston, A. (2002). Marker correspondence, not processing latency, determines temporal binding of visual attributes. *Current Biology, 12,* 359–368.

Viviani, P., & Aymoz, C. (2001). Color, form, and movement are not perceived simultaneously. *Vision Research, 41,* 2909–2918.

Perceptual latency priming

Temporal order judgments and reaction time measurements are methods to study the speed with which a sensory stimulus becomes represented in awareness as a conscious sensation or conscious perception. Perceptual latency usually ranges between 0.05 and 0.15 s, depending on the state of the observer, intensity of the stimulus, method of measurement, and other factors. It has been discovered that the latency with which a target-object becomes registered in awareness can be shortened by presenting another object (a *prime*) immediately before the target. This effect can be called perceptual latency priming. Importantly, perceptual latency priming can be caused also by primes that themselves are masked by the following target, so that the primes have become invisible. In a typical perceptual latency priming study, perceptual latency for the target is measured in two conditions: (1) a control condition, where the target is presented without the prime; and (2) a main condition, where a priming stimulus is presented before the target. Effective primes can be presented at exactly the same location as the targets or at closely adjacent spatial areas. Onsets of primes usually precede onsets of targets by about 0.03–0.06 s. The temporal value of the facilitation effect in perceptual latency priming has been found to range from few milliseconds up to several dozen milliseconds. See also *masking**.

References

Bachmann, T. (1989). Microgenesis as traced by the successive paired-forms paradigm. *Acta Psychologica, 70,* 3–17.

Klotz, W., & Wolff, P. (1995). The effect of a masked stimulus on the response to the masking stimulus. *Psychological Research/Psychologische Forschung, 58,* 92–101.

Neumann, O. (1982). *Experimente zum Fehrer-Raab Effekt und das Wetterwart-Modell der visuellen Maskierung*. (Bericht Nr. 24/1982). Bochum, Germany: Psychologisches Institut der Ruhr-Universität Bochum, Arbeitseinheit Kognitionspsychologie.

Neumann, O., & Scharlau, I. (2006). Experiments on the Fehrer-Raab effect and the 'Weather Station Model' of visual backward masking. *Psychological Research/Psychologische Forschung*, special issue (in press).

Scharlau, I. (2002). Leading, but not trailing, primes influence temporal order perception: Further evidence for an attentional account of perceptual latency priming. *Perception and Psychophysics, 64*, 1346–1360.

Scharlau, I. (2004). Evidence against response bias in temporal order tasks with attention manipulation by masked primes. *Psychological Research/Psychologische Forschung, 68*, 224–236.

Scharlau, I., and Neumann, O. (2003). Temporal parameters and time course of perceptual latency priming. *Acta Psychologica, 113*, 185–203.

Vorberg, D., Mattler, U., Heinecke, A., Schmidt, T., & Schwarzbach, J. (2003). Different time courses for visual perception and action priming. *Proceedings of the National Academy of Sciences USA, 100*, 6275–6280.

Perky effect

In this effect, a sensation produced by a real stimulus is misinterpreted as a (part of the) mental image by an observer who is engaged in a mental imagery task. Based on this effect, mental imagery can be modified and guided by the attributes and properties of the actual physical stimuli (e.g., size, orientation, and color), even when the stimuli are perceptually subliminal. On the other hand, if such a mental image is effectively formed (and possibly modified by the actual sensory stimulus), it can mask the sensory stimulus, which otherwise, when the imagery-instruction is not given, would be sensed as an external stimulus without difficulty. The effect was first described by Cheves West Perky (1874–1940) in 1910 when she was a postgraduate student of Edward Titchener.

Reference

Perky, C. W. (1910). An experimental study of imagination. *American Journal of Psychology, 21*, 422–425.

Phenomenal causality

In phenomenal causality, if one moving stimulus makes an impact with another visual stimulus and the latter changes its momentum (e.g., begins to move, changes speed or direction of motion), observers experience this event as if the first stimulus were the cause of the change in the second stimulus. The events are perceived to be causally linked. The *launching effect* is perceived when the movement or change in motion of the second object is simultaneous with the impact or is delayed by only a small time interval, for example, 50–100 ms (*delayed launching effect*). The perception of the immediate causality becomes difficult if the time interval is increased beyond about 100 ms. In that case, observers perceive the movement or the change in movement of the second object as caused by a kind of independent initiative. If the inducing object stops short of the induced object without contacting it, phenomenal causality can be still perceived; the higher the speed of motion of the causing agent, the larger is the spatial distance allowing the causal effect to be perceived. It is noteworthy that even unrelated events appear to be causally related if they immediately follow one another: for example, a truck passing a pond and lightning striking the same pond a fraction of a second later. In the stream/bounce display, two objects move toward each other, coincide, and then move apart. This event is perceptually *multistable*: observers perceive either bouncing or streaming of objects through each other.

Interestingly, phenomenal causality can be perceived also with intermodal displays. Moreover, a brief sound at the moment of contact induces bouncing as the dominant version of how stream/bounce displays are experienced. See also *tunnel effect**, *anthropomorphic perception effect**.

References

Guski, R., & Troje, N. (2003). Audiovisual phenomenal causality. *Perception and Psychophysics, 65*, 789–800.
Michotte, A. (1963). *The perception of causality.* New York: Basic Books.
Rock, I. (1975). *An introduction to perception.* New York: Macmillan.
Scholl, B. J., & Tremoulet, P. D. (2000). Perceptual causality and animacy. *Trends in Cognitive Sciences, 4*, 299–309.
Sekuler, R., Sekuler, A., & Lau, R. (1997). Sound alters visual motion perception. *Nature, 385*, 308.
Thinès, G., Costall, A., & Butterworth, G. (Eds.) (1991). *Michotte's experimental phenomenology of perception.* Hillsdale, NJ: Erlbaum.

Phonemic restoration effect

If a single phoneme is eliminated from a sentence and replaced with some brief nonphonemic auditory stimulus (a click or a very brief burst of noise), the listener is not aware that some important sound is missing from the words. The nonphonemic sound nevertheless can be heard, but out of its precise temporal location. Thus, phonemic restoration effect involves both a *negative illusion* and a true illusion of temporal misplacement.

Phosphenes

Phosphenes are the visual experiences that are produced by nonphotic (i.e., not depending on visible light) stimulation. One can consider effects caused by such influences as mechanical pressure on the eyeball, an object hitting the skull, direct effects of stimulating the exposed cortex (e.g., in the course of open-skull brain surgery), internal physiological effects different from normal neural processes projecting through the visual pathways (e.g., migraine headache phosphenes), transcranial magnetic stimulation effects, electrical effects via microelectrodes, and so forth. A large variety of phosphenes can occur in terms of their vividness, duration, repetitiveness, form, color and size. They can vary from tiny sparkle-like local flashes to mosaic-like colored patterns; checkerboard-like structures; spirals; bull's-eyes; hazy light; flickering light; blue, green, or red disks; wheel-like objects; star-like objects; flame-like perceptions; and so on. Anatomically, occipital primary visual areas and temporal areas in the cortex tend to be the locations where phosphenes can be evoked easily. At an eccentricity of the visual field about 10–20 deg from fixation, the phosphenes most often take the form of small spots. At larger eccentricities, cloud-like experiences often are reported. The most promising method of studying artificially evoked conscious experiences in normal observers capitalizes on the transcranial magnetic stimulation (TMS) methodology (e.g., see Walsh & Pascual-Leone, 2003; Kamitani & Shimojo, 1999). Occipital stimulation often leads to cuneiform shapes and also to shapes such as flashes, stripes, moving clouds, and circles. If small primary cortical visual (V1) stimulation is combined with frontal stimulation, achromatic experiences, bundles of lines, curved lines, sawtooth patterns, bands, then large dots frequently are reported. One-pulse TMS does not always lead to evoked phosphenes. Repetitive TMS is much more effective. Interestingly, parietal stimulation does not cause phosphenes, compared to the frequent phosphene-effects with visual-cortex and temporal-cortex stimulation. Colored phosphenes also can be experienced, with yellow and green being more frequent experiences than those of other colors.

References

Amassian, V. E., Cracco, R. Q., Maccabee, P. J., & Cracco, J. B. (2002). Visual systems. In A. Pascual-Leone, N. Davey, J. Rothwell, E. Wasserman, B. K. Puri (Eds.), *Handbook of transcranial magnetic stimulation* (pp. 323–334). London: Arnold.

Barker, A. T., Freeston, I. L., Jalinous, R., Merton, P. A., & Morton, H. B. (1985). Magnetic stimulation of the human brain. *Journal of Physiology, 369,* 3P.

Brindley, G. A., & Lewin, W. S. (1968). The sensations produced by electrical stimulation of the visual cortex. *Journal of Physiology, 196,* 479–493.

Dobelle, W. H., Mladejovski, M. G., & Girvin, J. P. (1974). Artificial vision for the blind: Electrical stimulation of visual cortex offers hope for a functional prosthetics. *Science, 183,* 440–443.

Kamitani, Y., & Shimojo, S. (1999). Manifestation of scotomas created by transcranial magnetic stimulation of human visual cortex. *Nature Neuroscience, 2,* 767–771.

Oster, G. (1970). Phosphenes. *Scientific American, 222,* 82–87.

Penfield, W. (1975). *The mystery of the mind.* Princeton, NJ: Princeton University Press.

Penfield, W., & Perot, P. (1963). The brain's record of auditory and visual experience: A final summary and discussion. *Brain, 86,* 595–696.

Tyler, C. W. (1978). Some new entopic phenomena. *Vision Research, 18,* 1633–1639.

Walsh, V., & Pascual-Leone, A. (2003). *Trans-cranial magnetic stimulation: A neurochronometrics of mind.* Cambridge, MA: MIT Press/Bradford.

Pop-out effects

In visual search paradigms, observers look for target-objects among several irrelevant (distractor) objects. The efficiency of the search depends on the type of features that distinguish target items from distractor items. For instance, on a gray background, a black target can be detected in a seemingly effortless manner and rapidly so when the distractors are all white, regardless of how many distractors are present. The targets that are defined by features that allow them to be found extremely fast and seemingly in an effortless manner are called *pop-out targets,* and the respective effects are called *pop-out effects.* The pop-out manner of noticing targets means that the time it takes to find the target is largely independent of the number of distractors. This suggests that all individual tests for each stimulus item's feature identity can be performed at the same time; that is, the search is *parallel.* Some typical pop-out features are a target's orientation or curvature of edges or lines, which clearly distinguish it from the respective orientations or curvatures of all of the distractors (e.g., target heavily tilted to the left, while nontargets are all vertical, or a single curved arc among nontarget straight-line segments; see Figure 31, left panel); the presence of distinct size differences between the target and distractors; the unique and easily discriminable color of the target compared to the uniform and different color of the distractors (e.g., the target is the only yellow object among the uniformly blue distractors); a target moving among stationary nontargets; a target having high brightness or contrast among distractors of lower brightness or contrast; a target whose shading indicates a convex protrusion among distractor items, whose reverse shading indicates a concave hole (see Figure 31, right panel).

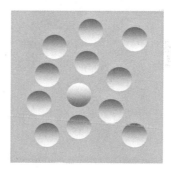

Figure 31

References

Folk, C. L., & Gibson, B. S. (Eds.). (2001). *Attraction, distraction, and action*. Amsterdam: Elsevier/North-Holland.

Treisman, A. M. (1986). Properties, parts, and objects. In K. R. Boff, L. Kaufman, & J. P. Thomas (Eds.), *Handbook of perception and human performance* (Vol. 2; pp. 35.1–35.70). New York: Wiley.

Wolfe, J. M. (1998). Visual search. In H. Pashler (Ed.), *Attention* (pp. 13–73). Hove, England: Psychology Press.

Prism adaptation effects

A person wearing wedge-shaped prism spectacles, resulting in displacement of the visual field objects and features to one side (e.g., displacement for 10 deg) becomes adapted to this displacement, so that normal body movements are possible and reaching out for objects in space is executed correctly. See also *inverted vision effects**.

Proactive contrast facilitation

Subjective contrast of a brief visual target-stimulus is enhanced when it is preceded by another brief (priming-) stimulus from the same or adjacent spatial location, compared to the subjective contrast of the target when it is presented alone. The optimum time intervals between the onsets of the prime and the target are approximately 40–100 ms. The effect is analogous to the *perceptual latency priming** effect.

References

Bachmann, T. (1988). Time course of the subjective contrast enhancement for a second stimulus in successively paired above-threshold transient forms: Perceptual retouch instead of forward masking. *Vision Research, 28,* 1255–1261.

Shchadrin, V. E., & Bongard, M. M. (1971). A new type of lateral interaction in the human visual system. *Vision Research, 11,* 241–249.

Pulfrich effect

Under normal viewing conditions, a pendulum swinging in a frontoparallel plane is perceived veridically to move along a planar trajectory. However, when an achromatic optical filter is placed before one of the eyes, the pendulum appears to move along an elliptical path in depth. The most likely explanation for this effect states that, because the signals from the eye that is covered by the filter are weaker than the signals from the other eye, it takes more time for them to be processed up to the cortical levels of analysis. This temporal lag translates into a spatial lag relative to the signals from the other eye. In other words, for a moving object like the pendulum, the relative temporal delay between the signals coming from the two eyes translates into a spatial offset between their retinotopic positions in the cortex. In effect, a binocular image disparity is produced that in turn yields a stereoscopic effect (movement in depth). The effect was described by Carl P. Pulfrich (1858–1927) in 1922. See also *flash-lag effect** and *Hess effect**.

References

Pulfrich, C. (1922). Die Stereoscopie im Dienste der isochromen und heterochromen Photometrie. *Naturwissenschaften, 10,* 553–564.

Rogers, B. J., & Anstis, S. M. (1972). Intensity versus adaptation and the Pulfrich stereophenomenon. *Vision Research, 12,* 909–928.

Repetition blindness

When observers have to detect a target-object within a stream of rapidly presented, spatially overlapping distractor objects, they often miss the second presentation of the target, provided that it follows the first presentation within about 200 to 400 ms. This effect, *repetition blindness*, occurs with stimuli such as words, letters, numerals, and forms. Rapid serial visual presentation conditions (RSVP streams) are usually necessary to induce repetition blindness. The rate of presentation of the items in a stream allowing the repetition blindness effect to occur is about 6–12 items per s (i.e., stimulus onset asynchrony between successive items about 80–160 ms). The best-known explanation of the repetition blindness effect assumes that the items have to be processed both for their identity and also differentiated from the rest of stimulation as instances of distinct objects (individuated as tokens). Repetition blindness is hypothesized to represent target identification without token individuation for its second occurrence. See also *attentional blink*.

References

Chun, M. M. (1997). Types and tokens in visual processing: A double-dissociation between the attentional blink and repetition blindness. *Journal of Experimental Psychology: Human Perception and Performance, 23,* 738–755.

Fagot, C., & Pashler, H. E. (1995). Repetition blindness: Perception or memory failure? *Journal of Experimental Psychology: Human Perception and Performance, 21,* 275–292.

Hochhaus, L., & Johnston, J. C. (1996). Perceptual repetition blindness effects. *Journal of Experimental Psychology: Human Perception and Performance, 22,* 355–366.

Kanwisher, N. (1987). Repetition blindness: Type recognition without token individuation. *Cognition, 27,* 117–143.

Representational momentum

The perceived final position of a moving and then suddenly vanishing target-object is displaced from its actual physical final position in the direction of motion. See also *Fröhlich effect*, *phenomenal causality*, *tunnel effect*, *stroboscopic motion*, *flash-lag effect*, *illusion*.

References

Freyd, J. J., & Finke, R. A. (1984). Representational momentum. *Journal of Experimental Psychology: Learning, Memory, and Cognition, 10,* 126–132.

Hubbard, T. L. (1995). Environmental invariants in the representation of motion: Implied dynamics and representational momentum, gravity, friction, and centripetal force. *Psychonomic Bulletin and Review, 2,* 322–338.

Müsseler, J., Stork, S., & Kerzel, D. (2002). Comparing mislocalizations with moving stimuli: The Fröhlich effect, the flash-lag effect and representational momentum. *Visual Cognition, 9,* 120–138.

Thornton, I. M., & Hubbard, T. L. (Eds.). (2002). *Representational momentum. New findings, new directions.* New York: Psychology Press/Taylor & Francis.

Repulsion effects

In visual perception and attention, there are several effects implying a kind of repulsion. The two best-known ones are *onset repulsion effect* and *attentional repulsion effect*. In the onset repulsion effect, the perceived starting point of a moving object is shifted phenomenally onto a position that was never physically occupied by that object, that is, in the opposite direction from the direction of movement. This effect is opposite to the *Fröhlich effect**, and whether one or the other effect takes place may depend on how far the stimuli are from the edge of the window in which they are displayed. In the attentional repulsion effect, when attention is focused onto some spatial location by the brief precue, the probe stimulus that appears subsequently at the cued location appears to be displaced away from the exact focus of attention. The attentional repulsion effect is best expressed when the probe stimuli are brief (e.g., less than 200 ms). See also *phenomenal causality**, *Fröhlich effect**, *Michotte effect, covert spatial attention effect**.

References

Hubbard, T. L., & Motes, M. A. (2002). Memory for initial position: A Fröhlich effect or an onset repulsion effect? *Journal of Vision, 2,* 28a.

Pratt, J., & Turk-Browne, N. B. (2003). The attentional repulsion effect in perception and action. *Experimental Brain Research, 152,* 376–382.

Suzuki, S., & Cavanagh, P. (1997). Focused attention distorts visual space: An attentional repulsion effect. *Journal of Experimental Psychology: Human Perception and Performance, 23,* 443–463.

Thornton, I. M. (2002). The onset repulsion effect. *Spatial Vision, 15,* 219–243.

Reversible figures

See *figure-ground reversal**, *ambiguous figures**, *multistability**.

Semantic satiation

When a word is repeated over and over again to an observer for a prolonged period ranging from tens of seconds to several minutes, at some moment in the repetition sequence, the observer will experience a loss of meaning of this word, although the utterances still signal the distinct and complete set of phonemic features pertaining to the sounds that form this word. Quite often, the word that is multiply repeated acquires a different experienced meaning from that of the initial one. Meaning transformation is easier with some words than with others. In some cases, the otherwise common and well-known word becomes experienced as funny or unfamiliar. A similar effect occurs when a written word is steadily inspected for a long time. The effect of semantic satiation occurs more easily when the observer is tired or fatigued. The phenomenon of semantic satiation demonstrates a kind of aversion of the consciousness mechanisms toward highly predictable and redundant stimulation while, in contrast, seeking novel and changing, that is, informative, stimulation. Compare also with *fading effects** and *stabilized images**.

References

Esposito, N. J., & Pelton, L. H. (1971). Review of the measurement of semantic satiation. *Psychological Bulletin, 75,* 330–346.
Severance, E., & Washburn, M. F. (1907). The loss of associative power in words after long fixation. *American Journal of Psychology, 18,* 182–186.

Sensory deprivation effects

When artificial conditions are used so that the sensory stimulation that an observer receives is reduced to a minimal possible level for some time (e.g., many minutes or hours), a set of physiological, perceptual, and cognitive effects are observed. First, observers usually sooner or later fall asleep. Then, upon waking, unusual and unpleasant subjective states gradually emerge since the sense organs are greatly understimulated and the conditions of physiological and mental activity are thus deprived of normal environmental sensory referencing systems and arousal components. The emerging states include restlessness, anxiety, panic attacks, distortions of perception and illusory experiences, hallucinations, overreacting to even faint stimuli, and so forth. Observers experience a kind of *stimulus hunger,* that is, a strong need for whatever stimulation there may be available. After the sensory deprivation, when normal circumstances resume, observers may experience unusually vivid and enjoyable sensations and emotions, but also illusions. In less dramatic conditions of sensory isolation (unchanging and monotonous stimulation with no variety in the environment, such as in solitary confinement, spaceship or submarine cells, arctic expedition habitats, etc.), some of the effects similar to sensory deprivation may also emerge. Nevertheless, although sensory deprivation also implies an extreme, monotonous form of (non)stimulation, monotonous but sufficiently strong sensory stimulation leads to mental effects that are usually much less dramatic than the effects of deprivation. (The techniques used to create conditions for sensory deprivation include immersion into water that is as still as possible and whose temperature is maintained at the average body temperature corresponding to the resting physiological state; exclusion of visual and auditory stimulation, the absence of light and use of soundproof surroundings, the exclusion of distinct smells, breathing through a mask, the restriction of all movement as much as possible, etc.) See also *Ganzfeld*, adaptation, fading effects**.

References

Bexton, W. H., Heron, W., & Scott, T. H. (1954). Effects of decreased variation in the sensory environment. *Canadian Journal of Psychology, 8,* 70–76.

Schultz, D. P. (1965). *Sensory restriction: Effects on behavior.* New York: Academic Press.

Zubek, J. P. (Ed.). (1969). *Sensory deprivation: Fifteen years of research.* New York: Appleton-Century-Crofts.

Sequential blanking

This is a variety of *masking** and *metacontrast* where some of the serially flashed letters of a word or a pseudoword are visually suppressed as a result of the presentation of some other letters of the word. The spatiotemporal conditions of stimulus presentation optimal for sequential blanking may be as follows: for example, letters of the word *SOMER-SAULT* are presented successively, each for 10–20 ms, in the temporal order specified by the numbers that are spatially arranged in correspondence with the spatial positions of the letters in the word, that is, 7, 5, 9, 2, 1, 10, 4, 3, 8, 6. In these conditions, observers typically perceive something like: *S M S LT.* It is noteworthy that if the same letters are presented with the same duration but in the left-to-right sequence, the sequential blanking effect is absent or negligible, indicating that the left-to-right reading habit influences microgenesis of visual awareness.

Sequential blanking can also be obtained with sequentially flashed and spatially staggered adjacent patterns.

References

Mayzner, M. S., & Tresselt, M. E. (1970). Visual information processing with sequential inputs: A general model for sequential blanking. *Annals of the New York Academy of Sciences, 169,* 599–618.
Mayzner, M. S., Tresselt, M. E., & Helfer, M. S. (1967). A research strategy for studying certain effects of very fast sequential input rates on the visual system. *Psychonomic Monograph Supplements, 2,* 73–81.
Piéron, H. (1935). Les processus du métacontraste. *Journal de Psychologie Normale et Pathologique, 31,* 5–24.
Pollack, I. (1972). Visual discrimination of 'unseen' objects: Forced choice testing of Mayzner-Tresselt sequential blanking effects. *Perception and Psychophysics, 11,* 121–128.

Simultanagnosia

The inability to perceive, recognize, or describe several simultaneously present objects contained in the visual field, although each object alone can be perceived and recognized. This is often a symptom involved in *Balint's syndrome.*

Size transformation effects

When the controlled duration of briefly presented visual objects is gradually increased, observers typically report an increase in the apparent size of the physically invariant objects, followed by the apparent decrease of the size. Similarly, the optical illusions involving apparent size effects also develop microgenetically. The range of durations allowing these types of effects is from about a few tens up to a few hundreds of milliseconds.

References

Bachmann, T. (2000). *Microgenetic approach to the conscious mind.* Amsterdam: John Benjamins.
Holt-Hansen, K. (1975). Duration of experienced expansion and contraction of a circle. *Perceptual and Motor Skills, 41,* 507–518.
Nakatani, K. (1995). Microgenesis of the length perception of paired lines. *Psychological Research, 58,* 75–82.
Reynolds, R. I. (1978). The microgenetic development of the Ponzo and Zöllner illusions. *Perception and Psychophysics, 23,* 231–236.

Sound-induced illusory flash phenomenon

When a flash of light is accompanied by multiple, brief auditory beeps, the single flash is perceived as multiple flashes. For the optimum effect, temporal separation of the stimuli should not exceed 100 ms. Importantly, gamma-frequency (~ 40 Hz) components of oscillations in brain activity in the visual cortical regions accompany this illusory effect. This illusion is an instance of cross-modal, perceptual-inducing effects, where sensory stimuli of one modality change the quality of the sensations in another modality. See also *McGurk effect*, Galli effect**.

References

Bhattacharya, J., Shams, L., & Shimojo, S. (2002). Sound-induced illusory flash perception: Role of gamma band responses. *NeuroReport, 13*, 1727–1730.

Shams, L., Kamitani, Y., & Shimojo, S. (2000). What you see is what you hear. *Nature, 408*, 788.

Shams, L., Kamitani, Y., & Shimojo, S. (2002). Visual illusion induced by sound. *Cognitive Brain Research, 14*, 147–152.

Stabilized images

Usually, the visual world around us appears as a stable, clear, and continuously present environment (without any spatial or temporal interruptions). One of the reasons for this seamlessness and continuity relates to eye movements. Because of voluntary and/or involuntary changes of visual fixation carried out by the movements of the eyes, the images of the objects and stimuli projected onto the retinas change their location. This appears to be an important precondition for sustained visual awareness of these objects. When, by some special technique (e.g., microslides and microlenses mounted on the eyeball by an aluminum device and a suction cup, or compensatory relocation of the screen images controlled by the recorded eye-movement signals), the image is spatially stabilized on the retina, it takes only few seconds for the image to fade out of conscious awareness. In addition to the contours, the color of the image-defined object also fades out. After the initial fading, the image may reappear (and disappear and reappear haphazardly). Usually, the reappearance of the image is fragmentary, with fragments apparently consisting of meaningful parts and elements of the stabilized object and not just any of its random parts or areas. Exploratory and motor activity and sensory change seem to be important for the maintenance of the full-blown, stable, continuous perceptual awareness. Flickering the retinally stabilized images restores conscious vision of the images. In Figure 15, a gray disk with hazy semicontours is depicted on the lighter background. After staring at the central dark dot for some time, observers may notice the disappearance of the disk from awareness, and the former visible area of the disk becomes *filled in** with the brightness value of the surrounding background. This demonstration, a result of adaptation and effective filling-in due to the absence of the abrupt contours of the object (which would help avoid fading in normal looking conditions), allows one to experience an effect similar to the one occurring with retinally stabilized images. See also *fading effects**, *retinal stabilization, adaptation, Ganzfeld**, *semantic satiation**.

References

Ditchburn, R. W. (1973). *Eye movements and perception.* Oxford: Clarendon.
Pritchard, R. M., Heron, W., & Hebb, D. O. (1960). Visual perception approached by the method of stabilized images. *Canadian Journal of Psychology, 14,* 67–77.
Riggs, L. A., Ratliff, F., Cornsweet, J. C., & Cornsweet, T. N. (1953). The disappearance of steadily fixated visual test objects. *Journal of the Optical Society of America, 43,* 495–501.
Yarbus, A. L. (1967). *Eye movements and vision.* New York: Plenum Press.

Standing wave illusion of invisibility

See *masking**.

Stoper and Mansfield effect

When the presentation of a large, uniformly light disk is quickly followed by a brief presentation of a small light object (e.g., a triangle) on a dark background, so that this small object falls within the large disk, observers report seeing both the large light disk and the small light object within it. However, the immediate surrounding of the small object appears as a halo of dark around it, corresponding to the brightness quality of its background (see also Figure 24). This dark halo has a diffuse edge gradually growing over to the light quality of the large disk. The sensory quality of the preceding stimulus (such as the light disk) is suppressed in a localized region specified by the location of the following stimulus and its immediate surroundings. The time interval between the onsets of the successive stimuli which permits a good Stoper and Mansfield effect to be experienced may equal about 80 to 100 ms. The effect is present also with dichoptic stimulation, where the stimuli are presented to different eyes. This suggests cortical loci for the effect. See also *brightness assimilation*, color spreading, halo effect*, filling-in*, masking**.

References

Motoyoshi, I. (1999). Texture filling-in and texture segregation revealed by transient masking. *Vision Research, 39,* 1285–1291.

Paradiso, M. A., & Nakayama, K. (1991). Brightness perception and filling in. *Vision Research, 31,* 1221–1236.

Stoper, A. E., & Mansfield, J. G. (1978). Metacontrast and paracontrast suppression of a contourless area. *Vision Research, 18,* 1669–1674.

Stroboscopic motion

If 2 (or more) spatially separated stimuli are successively flashed at an optimum time interval, observers experience motion of a single object instead of the perception of 2 (or more) different static objects. Apparent stroboscopic motion is perceived as beginning from the location of the first-flashed object and proceeding to the location of the second-flashed object. Importantly, virtually all animation in modern technology, such as in motion pictures (films, cinematography), television programs, computer-screen animation, and so forth, is based on this effect: the static frames of object images and scenes, presented at an optimal frame rate and with coherent frame-to-frame shifts in spatial position, create a dramatic experience of motion and animation dynamics. As Hans Eysenck has put it: "A well-known psychologist was once asked by a sceptical journalist to name a single psychological phenomenon on whose existence there was any agreement among psychologists, and the laws regarding which were sufficiently well known to make it of practical usefulness. He replied that not only was there such a phenomenon, but that it was so highly regarded by modern man that temples were put up to it in every town and village and that millions of people went to these temples every week, paying large sums of money in order to be admitted to view this phenomenon. The journalist was rather taken aback, until he realized that the psychologist was talking about the cinema" (Eysenck, 1965, p. 35).

The early students of stroboscopic movement, mostly the representatives of the Gestalt school of psychology, referred to these illusory experiences of motion as the *phi-phenomena* (e.g., Wertheimer, 1912). For stroboscopic movement phenomena to be easily observed, quite short duration flashes of the stimulus-objects should be used (e.g., 10 ms or 16.7 ms, as is typical for many computer-screen refresh rates of 60 Hz). Most of what has been discussed in the classical works on stroboscopic motion belongs to the domain of the so-called long-range apparent motion displays, where spatial separations between the successively flashed stimuli are in the range from a few dozen arc minutes up to many degrees of visual angle. (The so-called short-range apparent motion, which is typical for cinematographic images and random-dot kinematograms, involves spatial separations of about 5–20 min and time intervals of about 20–80 ms.)

If the perceptual quality of apparent motion is so good that observers find it difficult to discriminate it from the real motion of an otherwise identical object (i.e., one and the same object changing its location), it is termed *beta-motion*. Most often, and provided that optimal distances, sizes, and brightness levels characterize the objects, good motion is experienced with 50–80 ms time intervals between the onsets of the successive stimuli. With above-optimum time intervals, around 80–200 ms, a faint sensation of movement between the 2 (or more) objects can be experienced (objectless movement, where "something moves"). With below-optimum time intervals, partial apparent movement occurs, where it seems that the first-flashed object moves a bit toward the second object, and the second object seems itself also to move a bit before arriving at its final location. Naturally, with too-short time intervals, the objects appear as simultaneous; and with too-long intervals, the objects appear as 2 stationary stimuli in clear succession but without any sensation of movement. If the second-flashed stimulus is much more intense (bright) than the first-flashed stimulus, a reversed motion (*delta-motion*) may be experienced, where the movement seems to begin from the second-flashed object and proceed toward the first-flashed object.

If two objects that are successively flashed have different forms, apparent motion is more difficult (and, on rare occasions, impossible) to generate. If the sizes and formal aspects of the objects are optimal, a plastic transformation between the two shapes, that is, a *shape-morphing*, appears to take place along the motion path. If an object in the first frame is followed in the second frame by 2 equidistant objects, for example, to its left and right, the observer may perceive from trial to trial a leftward, a rightward, as well as a split motion, where the central object moves in both directions. These alternate perceptions can be modulated by varying the figural similarity between the objects. The visual system will favor the direction that helps maintain the figural identity or similarity between the objects that generate stroboscopic motion (*figural selection*). Because of the phenomenon of figural selection, motion pictures can be perceived as coherent and meaningful, without an unintelligible noise impression being created.

Stroboscopic motion is characterized by regularities (including the so-called *Korte's laws*) that relate the main stimulus attributes and properties governing the appearance of apparent motion with each other in a meaningful way. This helps to predict probabilities and qualities of the expected motion experiences. For instance, the larger the spatial distances by which the flashed stimuli are separated, the longer the time interval between their onsets has to be in order to lead to good apparent motion. Conversely, the larger the time interval, the larger the spatial separation has to be for a good motion. The longer the duration of 1 flashed object, the closer in time the following object has to be presented (the inter-stimulus interval must be shortened) in order to obtain a good motion percept. With an invariant time interval, the higher the intensity of the stimuli, the larger the spatial distance for good motion. With an invariant (fixed) spatial separation, the longer the time interval, the smaller the intensity has to be for optimal motion. These laws define a limit range of stimulus-variable values within which they hold. For instance, time intervals cannot be extended beyond a fraction of a second. The limits of space intervals are much more flexible and can extend to large spatial separations.

The long-range apparent-movement systems can be affected by cognitive control factors and are susceptible to attentional modulations. This is evidenced by the effects of set and expectancy on the resolution of multivalent apparent-movement alternatives, by the effects of spatial attention on the quality and direction of motion, by the effects of the meaning of the objects involved in stroboscopic motion on the direction and quality of motion, and so forth. See also *color-phi phenomenon**, *path-guided motion**, *Czermak effect**, *Ternus-Pikler effect**, *phenomenal causality**, *line-motion effect**.

References

Anstis, S. (1986). Motion perception in the frontal plane. In K. R.Boff, L. Kaufman, & J. P. Thomas (Eds.), *Handbook of perception and human performance. Vol. 1: Sensory processes and perception* (pp. 16.1–16.27). New York: John Wiley.

Exner, S. (1875). Experimentelle Untersuchung der einfachsten psychischen Processe. *Pflüger's Archiv für die gesamte Physiologie der Menschen und der Thiere, 11*, 403–432.

Eysenck, H. J. (1965). *Fact and fiction in psychology.* Harmondsworth, England: Penguin.

Kolers, P. A. (1972). *Aspects of motion perception.* Oxford: Pergamon.

Korte, A. (1915). Kinematoskopische Untersuchungen. *Zeitschrift für Psychologie, 72,* 193–296.

Wertheimer, M. (1912). Experimentelle Studien über das Sehen von Bewegung. *Zeitschrift für Psychologie, 61,* 161–265.

Subjective contours

See *illusory contours**.

Subjective rhythm

The succession of stimuli having objectively equal durations can be subjectively perceived in variable ways as forming subgroups of 2, 3, 4, or 5 stimuli. A subjectively perceived or produced accentuation (stress, emphasis) on the first one of the elements of each subgroup is the means to define and measure subjective grouping in creating subjective rhythm. The optimum interval between the successive stimuli which allows easy and variable subjective rhythm is about 750 ms. With time intervals between the successive stimuli less than 100–200 ms, subjective rhythm tends to become impossible. When increasing the time interval between the successive stimuli from 200 to 700 ms, the initially preferred paired rhythm tends to be replaced by triple- or quadruple-grouped rhythm. Several early classic psychologists, such as W. Wundt, F. Meumann, T. Bolton, and G. Dietze, already explored the phenomena of subjective rhythm. More recent researchers include Paul Fraisse, Robert Ornstein, John Michon, Dan Zakay, and others. In subjective grouping, the time intervals between the groups appear as being longer compared to the intervals between the neighboring elements of the same group. The task of synchronizing one's own movements (e.g., taps) with the periodic rhythmic stimulation (e.g., a metronome) is relatively easy if the time intervals between the stimuli are 200 to 1000 ms but difficult with a faster or a slower pace.

References

Fraisse, P. (1963). *The psychology of time.* New York: Harper & Row.

Michon, J. A., & Jackson, J. L. (1985). *Time, mind and behavior.* Berlin: Springer.

Ornstein, R. (1975). *On the experience of time.* Harmondsworth, England: Penguin.

Zakay, D., Nitzan, D., & Glicksohn, J. (1983). The influence of task difficulty and external tempo on subjective time estimation. *Perception and Psychophysics, 14,* 451–456.

Subjective stroboscopy

See *wagon-wheel illusion**.

Substitution masking

See *masking**.

Synesthesia (Synaesthesia)

A blending of sensory features from several modalities, when a stimulus that typically evokes a sensation in only one modality is presented. Examples are the sensations of different colors accompanying the presentation (and hearing) of correspondingly different tones, the seeing of colors accompanying black-on-white printed numbers, sensations of taste elicited by specific visual shapes, and so on. Evidence from brain activation patterns of synesthesic observers which differ from those of control observers suggests that systematic differences between the higher-level organization of sensory areas in their respective brains may contribute to synesthesia.

References

Cytowic, R. E. (1993). *The man who tasted shapes*. Cambridge, MA: MIT Press.
Hubbard, E. M., & Ramachandran, V. S. (2005). Neurocogntive mechanisms of synesthesia. *Neuron, 48,* 509–520.
Nunn, J. A., Gregory, L. J., Brammer, M., Williams, S. C., Parslow, D. M., Morgan, M. J., et al. (2002). Functional magnetic resonance imaging of synesthesia: Activation of V4/V8 by spoken words. *Nature Neuroscience, 5,* 371–375.
Ramachandran, V. S., & Hubbard, E. M. (2003). The phenomenology of synesthesia. *Journal of Consciousness Studies, 10,* 49–57.
Robertson, L. C., & Sagiv, N. (2005). *Synesthesia: Perspectives from cognitive neuroscience*. Oxford: Oxford University Press.

Tandem effect

When a pair of horizontally separated and occluded objects that move in the horizontal direction becomes displayed in an aperture that has a horizontal diameter less than the inter-object distance, observers never-theless experience it as if they are seeing both objects at once in the aperture (Müsseler & Neumann, 1992). Factually, only one object at a time is present in the spatial window; introspectively, however, a pair is seen. The effect appears with optimum speed of motion and optimum inter-object distance. The tandem effect can be explained by any of the different variety of the two-process theories of conscious perception: the first stimulus that appears from behind the occluding surface opens two processes—preconscious perceptual encoding and a slower process of attention (or *nonspecific thalamic modulation*)—that are necessary for explicit perception; the following stimulus's explicit perception is accel-erated because its encoding benefits from the attention-shifting or mod-ulatory process initiated by the first stimulus, and thus, it becomes ex plicitly perceived faster than the first stimulus, which did not have a preceding, attention-evoking event. This leads to the compression of the subjectively evaluated distance between the stimuli. See also *Fröh-lich effect*, anorthoscopic perception*, flash-lag effect*, Zöllner effect**.

References

Bachmann, T. (1997). Visibility of brief images: The dual-process approach. *Consciousness and Cognition, 6,* 491–518.
Müsseler, J., & Neumann, O. (1992). Apparent distance reduction with moving stimuli (tandem effect): Evidence for an attention-shifting model. *Psychological Research/Psychologische Forschung, 54,* 246–266.

Temporal context effect of brightness

In this effect, temporal relations of spatially adjacent objects modulate the perceived brightnesses of the objects. For instance, if two flashes are presented on either side of a fixation dot, one for a long duration (e.g., over 200 ms) and the other for a short duration (e.g., 60 ms), observers will report that the brightnesses of the two flashes depend on their tem-poral relationship. When the two flashes are temporally arranged to have simultaneous onsets, the brief flash appears dimmer. When the two flashes are arranged to have simultaneous offsets, the brief flash ap-pears brighter.

Reference

Eagleman, D. M., Jacobson, J. E., & Sejnowski, T. J. (2004). Perceived lumi-nance depends on temporal context. *Nature, 428,* 854–856.

Temporal order reversal effect

When two very brief and spatially overlapping visual objects are presented in rapid succession with the first object having a higher contrast than the succeeding object, then observers perceive the illusory reversal of temporal order (Bachmann, Põder, & Luiga, 2004). The stimulus that was presented as the first appears to be presented as the second. The time intervals between the onsets of the stimuli enabling illusory order reversal should be shorter than about 50 ms. The temporal order reversal effect seems to be a perceptual bias effect, because if the two spatially superimposed stimuli that have clearly different contrast are presented simultaneously, the higher-contrast one nevertheless appears to be presented later than the lower-contrast stimulus.

Reference

Bachmann, T., Põder, E., & Luiga, I. (2004). Illusory reversal of temporal order: The bias to report a dimmer stimulus as the first. *Vision Research, 44,* 241–246.

Ternus-Pikler effect

An invariant display of the two three-element sets of stimuli may lead to two different experiences of *stroboscopic motion**, depending on the temporal interval and mindset of the observers. In his seminal study, Ternus (1926/1950) modified a stimulus configuration introduced earlier by Pikler (1917): 3 horizontally aligned dots A, B, C were presented in the first frame, and similar 3 dots B, C, D were presented in the second frame, so that B and C were spatially identical in both triplets, but A and D were present as unique elements (see Figure 32). Observers can experience *element motion*, where B and C are perceived as a static structure and A appears to jump over B and C to the position D. An alternative percept is *group motion*, where the triplet A, B, C seems to move in unison to the new position B, C, D, so that A moves to position B, B moves to position C, and C moves to position D. Element motion dominates when the time interval between the exposures of the groups is less than 50 to 60 ms; group motion is a dominant experience when the time interval is larger. The probability of seeing group motion increases with frame duration (thus allowing group-motion perception at shorter inter-stimulus intervals). If the superimposed elements (B, C) are slightly spatially shifted between the two frames, the probability of element motion decreases. Other variables that modulate the probability of seeing element/group motion include eccentricity, element geometry, element size, spatial organization, feature similarity, figural context, and relative depth. See also *feature attribution**.

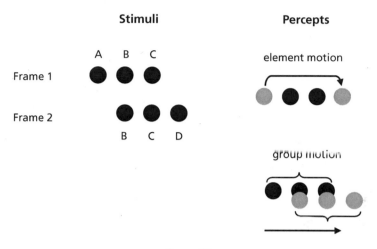

Stimuli   **Percepts**

Figure 32

References

Breitmeyer, B. G., & Ritter, A. (1986). Visual persistence and the effect of eccentric viewing, element size, and frame duration on bistable stroboscopic motion percepts. *Perception and Psychophysics, 39,* 275–280.

Dawson, M. R., Nevin-Meadows, N., & Wright, R. D. (1994). Polarity matching in the Ternus configuration. *Vision Research, 34,* 3347–3359.

Dawson, M. R., & Wright, R. D. (1994). Simultaneity in the Ternus configuration: Psychophysical data and a computational model. *Vision Research, 34,* 397–407.

Grossberg, S., & Rudd, M. E. (1989). A neural architecture for visual motion perception: Group and element apparent motion. *Neural Networks, 2,* 431–450.

He, Z. J., & Ooi, T. L. (1999). Perceptual organization of apparent motion in the Ternus display. *Perception, 28,* 877–892.

Kolers, P. A. (1972). *Aspects of motion perception.* Oxford: Pergamon Press.

Kramer, P., & Rudd, M. (1999). Visible persistence and form correspondence in Ternus apparent motion. *Perception and Psychophysics, 61,* 952–962.

Pantle, A. J., & Petersik, J. T. (1980). Effects of spatial parameters on the perceptual organization of a bistable motion display. *Perception and Psychophysics, 27,* 307–312.

Pantle, A., & Picciano, L. (1976). A multistable movement display: Evidence for two separate motion systems in human vision. *Science, 193,* 500–502.

Petersik, J. T. (1984). The perceptual fate of letters in two kinds of apparent movement displays. *Perception and Psychophysics, 36,* 146–150.

Petersik, J. T., Schellinger, A. R., & Geiger, S. L. (2003). Do variables that affect similar bistable apparent-movement displays result in similar changes in perception? *Spatial Vision, 16,* 105–123.

Pikler, J. (1917). *Sinnesphysiologische Untersuchungen.* Leipzig: Barth.

Scott-Samuel, N. E., & Hess, R. F. (2001). What does the Ternus display tell us about motion processing in human vision? *Perception, 30,* 1179–1188.

Ternus, J. (1926). Experimentelle Untersuchungen über phänomenale Identität. *Psychologische Forschung, 7,* 81–136.

Ternus, J. (1950). The problem of phenomenal identity. In Ellis, W. D. (Ed.), *A sourcebook of Gestalt psychology.* New York: Humanities Press.

Tip-of-the-tongue phenomenon

A phenomenon sometimes occurs when someone tries to retrieve from memory a specific word but fails, yet still has a feeling that she or he knows this word (e.g., a name) and is about to recall it. (It often happens with remembering surnames or specialist terms.) One is consciously aware of knowing *that* one has a relevant item of semantic/verbal knowledge *available* while, however, it remains *inaccessible* to awareness at the given moment. The emergence of the *feeling of knowing* the answer to a test question tends to predict subsequent correct recognition compared to the test questions that do not create this feeling. The adequacy of this experience can be proved by suggesting some wrong name to the observer, who is in the state of the tip-of-the-tongue experience; he or she immediately and correctly knows that what is suggested is a wrong answer. Therefore, the tip-of-the-tongue phenomenon must veridically tap some preconscious representations without assisting in opening these representations for explicit use and direct experience. Also, when the observer finally remembers the correct word, she or he immediately understands that the answer is the correct one. Typically, abandoning the attempts to retrieve the sought-after word for a while helps to retrieve it spontaneously at a later moment. Sometimes, some vague awareness of the form or an aspect of the sound of the unretrievable word accompanies the phenomenon. The tip-of-the-tongue phenomenon tends to occur more readily when some other well-remembered word surfaces in one's consciousness instead and it, rather than the to-be-remembered word, occupies the working memory store. This suggests that some form of suppression, such as lateral inhibition, acting within the hierarchically organized semantic/verbal representational system contributes to the tip-of-the-tongue phenomenon. This phenomenon tends to become more frequent with advancing age.

References

Brown, R., & McNeill, D. (1966). The tip-of-the-tongue phenomenon. *Journal of Verbal Learning and Verbal Behavior, 5,* 325–337.
Harley, T. A., & Brown, H. E. (1998). What causes a tip-of-the-tongue state? Evidence for lexical neighborhood effects in speech production. *British Journal of Psychology, 89,* 151–174.
Koriat, A. (1993). How do we know that we know? The accessibility model of feeling of knowing. *Psychological Review, 100,* 609–639.
Krinsky, R., & Krinsky, S. J. (1988). City size bias and the feeling of knowing. In M. M. Gruneberg, P. E. Morris, & R. N. Sykes (Eds.), *Practical aspects of memory: Current research and issues* (Vol. 1). Chichester, England: Wiley.

Tunnel effect

When a visible moving object disappears from sight (entering a "tunnel") and then reappears after having seemingly passed through the tunnel at its other end, observers often experience a ghostly motion of the object within the tunnel (Burke, 1952). For this *illusion** to occur, the time during which the object actually remains invisible (as if being hidden in the tunnel) should be rather short, for example, 15–40 ms. Interestingly, if the object moves into the tunnel with its movement path being directed also downward (e.g., from upper left to lower right), its illusory path within the tunnel appears as if the object possesses some inertia: at its lowest point, it reaches a location a bit lower in space than, and then regains the altitude within, the tunnel, in conformity with the altitude of the path that leads the object out of the tunnel. Illusory perception seems to follow the natural laws of movement and inertia. See also *stroboscopic motion**, *path-guided motion**, *phenomenal causality**.

References

Burke, L. (1952). On the tunnel effect. *Quarterly Journal of Experimental Psychology, 4,* 121–138.
Flombaum, J. I., & Scholl, B. J. (2006). A temporal same-object advantage in the tunnel effect: Facilitated change detection for persisting objects. *Journal of Experimental Psychology: Human Perception and Performance, 32,* 840–853.
Kawachi, Y., & Gyoba, J. (2006). A new response-time measure of object persistence in the tunnel effect. *Acta Psychologica, 123,* 73–90.

Tunnel vision

When vision is engaged in a quite effortful central task (e.g., discriminating rapidly consecutive symbols presented in central vision), and visual noise is introduced to the display, the effective visual field for additional stimulus detection narrows down considerably. The larger the processing load and effort, the stronger the tunnel-vision effect. Short exposure times accentuate tunnel vision.

Reference

Mackworth, N. H. (1965). Visual noise causes tunnel vision. *Psychonomic Science, 3,* 67–68.

Ventriloquist effect

See the *McGurk effect**.

Visuo-spatial hemi-neglect

A neurological syndrome, typically caused by unilateral parietal lobe damage, that renders the patient unresponsive to sensory stimuli presented in the contralateral visual field. Hemi-neglect is thought to be a type of pathological deficit of attention. Often, neglect is more profound with damage of the right as compared to left posterior parietal cortex. Visuo-spatial hemi-neglect is different from the *blindsight**; the early visual pathways and the primary visual cortex are intact, and the initial sensory processing of the signals is normal. In some cases, it appears as if and although an observer is literally seeing the object but, nevertheless, does not attend to it at all, investing null-interest in any higher-level perceptual and response-related processing to it. Also called *spatial hemi-neglect, unilateral neglect,* or simply *neglect.*

References

Bisiach, E., & Luzzatti, C. (1978). Unilateral neglect of representational space. *Cortex, 14,* 129–133.

Fahle, M. (2003). Failures of visual analysis: Scotoma, agnosia, and neglect. In M. Fahle & M. Greenlee (Eds.), *The neuropsychology of vision* (pp. 179–258). Oxford: Oxford University Press.

Heilman, K. M. (1979). Neglect and related disorders. In K. M. Heilman & E. Valenstein (Eds.), *Clinical neuropsychology* (pp. 268–307). New York: Oxford University Press.

Wagon-wheel illusion

Slight spatial displacements of an object in successive frames of a movie create the perception of continuous motion (see *stroboscopic motion**). If the sampling frequency at which the frames of the movie are produced is too low with respect to the rotation frequency of an object, the object appears to rotate backward, as illustrated by the classical example of apparently backward-rotating wagon wheels in the Western movie genre. As such, this phenomenon can be explained by *temporal aliasing* and *stroboscopic motion**. However, several studies reported that the same illusion can be observed under continuous lighting conditions. Because there is no physical undersampling in continuous-lighting wagon-wheel illusion (CLWWI), this version of the illusion has been interpreted to result from a sampling process occurring in the visual system (temporal sampling resulting from putative, discrete perceptual moments or spatial sampling in motion detectors). However, there are several differences between the wagon-wheel illusion and CLWWI. For example, while the perception of reversed motion is immediate in the wagon-wheel illusion, it may take several seconds and even minutes for the illusory percept to develop in CLWWI. The wagon-wheel illusion depends on the sampling Nyquist frequency; CLWWI, on the other hand, occurs only for a specific frequency range (2–20 Hz). In the wagon-wheel illusion, the perceived direction of motion is stable. In CLWWI, the perceived direction of motion is bi-stable, and the veridical direction dominates.

References

Andrews, T., & Purves, D. (2005). The wagon-wheel illusion in continuous light. *Trends in Cognitive Sciences, 9*, 261–263.

Schouten, J. F. (1967). Subjective stroboscopy and a model of visual movement detectors. In I. Wathen-Dunn (Ed.), *Models for the perception of speech and visual form* (pp. 44–45). Cambridge, MA: MIT Press.

Van Rullen, R. (2006). The continuous Wagon Wheel Illusion is object-based. *Vision Research, 46*, 4091–4095.

Van Rullen, R., Reddy, L., & Koch, C. (2006). The continuous wagon wheel illusion is associated with changes in electroencephalogram power at approximately 13 Hz. *Journal of Neuroscience, 26*, 502–507.

Zöllner (Zoellner) effect

In *anorthoscopic perception**, the apparent distance between the stimuli that move behind the occluder (and are revealed in the aperture only part by part at any one time) appears to be compressed in the direction of motion. Similar effects have been reported earlier by Plateau and Roget. (See also *tandem effect**.)

Reference

Plateau, J. (1836) Notice sur l'Anorthoscope. *Bulletin de l'Académie des Sciences et Belles Lettres de Bruxelles. 3*, 7–10.

Roget, P. M. (1825). Explanation of an optical deception in the appearance of the spokes of a wheel seen through vertical apertures. *Philosophical Transactions of the Royal Society of London, 115*, 131–140.

Zöllner, F. (1862). Über eine neue Art anorthoscopischer Zerrbilder. *Annalen der Physik und Chemie: Poggendorffs Annalen, 117*, 477–484.

Additional Terms

We suggest that readers should search for the explanations of or commentaries on the additional terms listed below in various dictionaries, encyclopedias, and handbooks devoted to psychology, neuroscience, and philosophy, as well as on the Internet. These terms also may be related to consciousness research issues; but compared to the terms provided as the main entries of this dictionary, they need not necessarily represent the phenomena or effects where consciousness (awareness) of the actual stimulation can be regarded as an experimental variable. Also, some effects are included in this list of additional terms that derive more from traditional cognitive psychology and psychophysics than from consciousness research as such. In some cases, laws or regularities that describe or categorize phenomena but are not phenomena per se are included.

Terms marked with an asterisk are listed and described in this dictionary; the terms in italics, but without asterisks, should be consulted about independently in other dictionaries or handbooks.

Adaptation effects
See *selective adaptation, brightness aftereffect, contrast aftereffect, motion aftereffect, tilt aftereffect, figural aftereffects*, negative afterimage*, complementary afterimage**.

Aftereffects
See *brightness aftereffect, contrast aftereffect, figural aftereffects*, motion aftereffect*, prism aftereffect*, selective adaptation*.

Afterimage
Positive afterimage, negative afterimage, complementary afterimage.

Ascending staircase effect

Bloch's law

Iconic memory
See also *positive afterimage*.

Kappa effect
See also *Tau (τ) effect.*

Korte's laws
See also *stroboscopic motion*, phi (φ) phenomena, apparent motion.*

Libet's effect
Also called *antedating.*

Object superiority effect (Weisstein-Harris effect)

Perceptual defense

Perceptual set effects
See, for example, Bruner and Goodman; Bruner and Postman.

Phantom limbs

Pötzl (Poetzl) effect
See also *subliminal perception, perceptual defense.*

Precedence effect

Prior-entry effect

Purkinje shift

Retinal adaptation effects
See *selective adaptation, fading effects*, stabilized images*, afterimages.*

Saccadic suppression

Selective adaptation effects
See also *adaptation, retinal adaptation, aftereffects.*

Shine-through effect

Simultaneous contrast
See also *contrast*, Mach bands, Benary effect*.*

Spiral aftereffect
See *aftereffects, motion aftereffect*, selective adaptation.*

Subliminal perception effects
See *implicit perception, masked object-priming*, perceptual latency-priming*.*

Successive contrast
See *complementary afterimage*.*

Tau effect
See also *Kappa (κ) effect.*

Temporal integration
See also *afterimage, masking*, Bloch's law.*

Thatcher illusion

Tickling paradox

Tilt aftereffect
See also *aftereffects, adaptation, figural aftereffect**.

Troxler effect
See also *fading effects**.

Uznadze effect
See also *intermodal Uznadze effect.*

Ventriloquism
See also *McGurk effect**.

Visual capture

Word-letter phenomenon

Word superiority effect (Reichert-Wheeler effect)

Name Index

Subject Index